T0328584

.

Cambridge Elements

Elements in the Philosophy of Mathematics
edited by
Penelope Rush
University of Tasmania
Stewart Shapiro
The Ohio State University

INDISPENSABILITY

A. C. Paseau
University of Oxford

Alan Baker
Swarthmore College

CAMBRIDGE
UNIVERSITY PRESS

Shaftesbury Road, Cambridge CB2 8EA, United Kingdom

One Liberty Plaza, 20th Floor, New York, NY 10006, USA

477 Williamstown Road, Port Melbourne, VIC 3207, Australia

314–321, 3rd Floor, Plot 3, Splendor Forum, Jasola District Centre, New Delhi – 110025, India

103 Penang Road, #05–06/07, Visioncrest Commercial, Singapore 238467

Cambridge University Press is part of Cambridge University Press & Assessment, a department of the University of Cambridge.

We share the University's mission to contribute to society through the pursuit of education, learning and research at the highest international levels of excellence.

www.cambridge.org
Information on this title: www.cambridge.org/9781009096850

DOI: 10.1017/9781009099042

First published 2023

A catalogue record for this publication is available from the British Library.

ISBN 978-1-009-09685-0 Paperback
ISSN 2399-2883 (online)
ISSN 2514-3808 (print)

Indispensability

Elements in the Philosophy of Mathematics

DOI: 10.1017/9781009099042
First published online: May 2023

A. C. Paseau
University of Oxford

Alan Baker
Swarthmore College

Author for correspondence: A. C. Paseau, paseau@maths.ox.ac.uk

Abstract: Our best scientific theories explain a wide range of empirical phenomena, make accurate predictions, and are widely believed. Since many of these theories make ample use of mathematics, it is natural to see them as confirming its truth. Perhaps the use of mathematics in science even gives us reason to believe in the existence of abstract mathematical objects such as numbers and sets. These issues lie at the heart of the Indispensability Argument, to which this Element is devoted. The Element's first half traces the evolution of the Indispensability Argument from its origins in Quine and Putnam's works, taking in naturalism, confirmational holism, Field's program, and the use of idealisations in science along the way. Its second half examines the explanatory version of the Indispensability Argument, and focuses on several more recent versions of easy-road and hard-road fictionalism respectively.

Keywords: Indispensability Argument, confirmational holism, nominalism, platonism, fictionalism

ISBNs: 9781009096850 (PB), 9781009099042 (OC)
ISSNs: 2399-2883 (online), 2514-3808 (print)

Contents

1 Introduction   1

2 Naturalism and Holism   4

3 Hard Road Nominalism: Field's Program   13

4 An Objection from Scientific Practice   22

5 The Enhanced Indispensability Argument   30

6 Easy Road Fictionalism   38

7 Hard Road Fictionalism   47

8 Conclusions   52

References   54

1 Introduction

Science cannot do without mathematics, so if you believe science, you had better believe mathematics. That, in lay terms, is the Indispensability Argument. The striking thing about this argument, which we will set out more formally shortly, is that it locates the justification for mathematics outside mathematics itself. Scientists develop theories about the physical world as varied as general relativity, the atomic theory of matter, Darwin's theory of evolution by natural selection, and many more. The best of these explain a wide range of empirical phenomena, make accurate predictions, and are widely believed. But not only that, goes the claim: to the extent that they use mathematics, such theories give us a reason for believing its truth. And even a cursory look at scientific theories shows how many of them use mathematics and how extensively. So we should believe mathematics.

Take the example of Fermat's Last Theorem: if positive integers n, x, y, and z are such that $x^n + y^n = z^n$ then $n = 1$ or $n = 2$. Following its proof by Andrew Wiles and Richard Taylor in the mid-1990s, mathematicians now accept the theorem as true. Indispensabilists maintain that we are justified in believing Fermat's Last Theorem because the axioms and rules needed to prove it are all justified by their utility to science. Science either needs these axioms and rules directly or needs mathematical claims best systematized in terms of them. Mathematics is indispensable to science because science cannot manage without it.

The Indispensability Argument is regularly said to be the strongest argument for believing in the truth of mathematics. And of course most philosophers, not to mention the overwhelming majority of mathematicians and laypeople, take mathematics to be true. In fact, even some philosophers who think (nonvacuous) mathematical claims are not true regard the Indispensability Argument as the main argument worth taking seriously. An example is Hartry Field, who in the preface to his book *Science Without Numbers* declares: "The only non-question-begging arguments I have ever heard for the view that mathematics is a body of truths all rest ultimately on the applicability of mathematics to the physical world; so if applicability to the physical world isn't a good argument either, then there is no reason to regard any part of mathematics as true" (Field 1980, p. viii).

The Indispensability Argument – in its present and classic version that applies to mathematics – is often called the "Quine–Putnam Indispensability Argument," after the Harvard philosophers W. V. Quine and Hilary Putnam. No exact formulation of the argument can be found in Quine's works, though loose versions of the idea certainly appear in them from the early 1950s onwards.

Putnam (1971) articulates the argument more precisely in his *Philosophy of Logic*.

The Indispensability Argument aims to establish the truth of mathematical claims, and thereby the existence of mathematical objects. One could question the inference from the truth of mathematical claims to the existence of mathematical objects, as Putnam himself did in a later incarnation, but we shall not do so here.[1] Following Colyvan (2001, p. 1), but with one small difference (see Footnote 7), we favor a two-premise version of the argument:[2]

The Indispensability Argument

1. We ought rationally to be ontologically committed to objects indispensable to our best scientific theories.
2. Mathematical objects are indispensable to our best scientific theories.

We ought rationally to be ontologically committed to mathematical objects.

Mathematical objects include numbers, sets, functions, groups, and the like. It is generally believed that if they exist, these objects are *abstract*, meaning, roughly, nonspatiotemporal and noncausal. In fact, mathematical objects serve as paradigms of abstract objects. Those who believe mathematical objects exist and are abstract are known as *platonists*. Platonists about a branch of mathematics take its accepted statements to be meaningful, declarative, and true, and construe them at face value as being about abstract objects. Platonists about arithmetic, for example, understand "11 is prime" as the claim that the abstract object 11 has the property of being prime. If we assume that mathematical objects are abstract,[3] the Indispensability Argument is then an argument for platonism.

Quine initially rejected platonism, and in fact believed no abstract objects exist, but later became a platonist on indispensability grounds. Early on in his career, he tried to regiment the mathematical parts of science so as to avoid commitment to mathematical, and thus abstract, objects. (He assumed that if mathematics contains

---

[1] See Paseau (2007) and chapter 7 of Paseau (forthcoming b). For Putnam, see Footnote 6. Pincock (2012, chapter 9) mentions other writers who have questioned this inference.

[2] Later, from Section 5 onwards, when there is another version of the argument to contrast it with, this original version of the argument will be known as the Quine–Putnam Indispensability Argument.

[3] This assumption is very common but not universal: see, for example, the "Aristotelian realism" defended in Franklin (2014).

reference to objects then they must be abstract.) He wrote a famous article with Nelson Goodman that sought to do this for some elementary portions of applied mathematics (Quine and Goodman 1947). For example, the statement

$$2 + 3 = 5$$

can be paraphrased as the logical truth

$$(\exists_2 x(Fx) \wedge \exists_3 x(Gx) \wedge \forall x \neg (Fx \wedge Gx)) \rightarrow \exists_5 x(Fx \vee Gx),$$

which may be read as "If there are exactly two Fs and exactly three Gs and nothing is both F and G then there are exactly five F-or-Gs." Here "$\exists_2 x(Fx)$" abbreviates

$$\exists x \exists y (Fx \wedge Fy \wedge x \neq y \wedge \forall z (Fz \rightarrow (z = x \vee z = y))),$$

which involves no reference to the number 2. Similarly for $\exists_3 x(Fx)$ and $\exists_5 x(Fx)$. Since the paraphrases contain no quantifiers ranging over a domain of abstract objects, nor singular terms denoting abstract objects, by Quine's lights, they harbor no commitment to such objects.[4]

And yet despite his best efforts, Quine came to the conclusion that this approach could not be made to work for nonelementary parts of mathematics that go far beyond such simple claims as $2 + 3 = 5$. Try as he might, he could not avoid reference to, or quantification over, mathematical objects. His apparent failure convinced him that it could not be done at all. With initial reluctance, he grasped the nettle and embraced the Indispensability Argument's second premise (in our terminology). He recanted his earlier wholesale rejection of the abstract and accepted abstract mathematical objects.[5]

Quine did not believe that the meanings of our scientific beliefs rigidly constrain regimentation. In this respect, he differed from Putnam, who was more interested in respecting the meaning of what "one daily presupposes" in the practice of science. The latter wrote:

> quantification over mathematical entities is indispensable for science, both formal and physical; therefore we should accept such quantification; but this commits us to accepting the existence of the mathematical entities in question. This type of argument stems, of course, from Quine, who has for years stressed both the indispensability of quantification over mathematical entities and the intellectual dishonesty of denying the existence of what one daily presupposes. (Putnam 1979, p. 347)

---

[4] Along with virtually all contemporary philosophers, we will assume throughout, mostly implicitly, something like these criteria of ontological commitment.

[5] But not any abstract objects beyond the mathematical. For example, he continued to reject meanings and propositions.

Putnam here states that the argument he puts forward "stems" from Quine, but whether Putnam ever believed that the Indispensability Argument established platonism about mathematics remains unclear.[6]

So much then for an introduction to the Indispensability Argument. We have stated the argument informally as well as more formally, and briefly reviewed its origins. Let us now trace some of the philosophical commitments behind the argument's premises before turning to more critical evaluation. The argument indisputably relies on naturalism for its plausibility and, more controversially, on confirmational holism. At any rate, both these principles were championed by Quine, in whose works the argument originated. We examine them in Section 2.

2 Naturalism and Holism

Naturalism is one of those catchwords, like freedom or democracy, that can mean virtually anything to anyone and in which just about everyone professes to believe. Adjectives help discipline the notion. According to *metaphysical* naturalism, the ontology of the world is in some sense "natural." Let us not dwell on what exactly that might mean, since it is another type of naturalism that is most relevant here: *methodological* naturalism. Methodological naturalism enjoins taking the epistemic standards/methods of the natural sciences as primary. As Quine (1981, p. 21) put it, "naturalism: the recognition that it is within science itself, and not in some prior philosophy, that reality is to be identified and described."

Quine never articulated methodological naturalism much more precisely. And he said little more about the scientific method than that it is made up of the norms of empirical adequacy and theoretical simplicity, scope, fertility, and familiarity. So what exactly might be meant by the primacy of scientific methods?

2.1 Methodological Naturalism

Here is a strong form of (methodological) naturalism:

> *Biconditional Naturalism*: One should believe *p* iff science endorses *p*.

By the term of art "science endorses *p*" we mean, roughly, that *p* follows from the tenets of a particular science along with observational statements via an

---

[6] See the later disavowal in Putnam (2012, pp. 181–3), where he backs away from ontological conclusions and even suggests that he never endorsed them. Putnam (1967) suggests that platonism and a non-platonist picture of mathematics (which later came to be known as "modal structuralism") are mathematically equivalent and equally satisfactory overall (though in some contexts one may be preferable to the other). Liggins (2008) expands on the differences between Quine and Putnam's versions of the Indispensability Argument, as does Putnam (2012) himself in chapter 9. Colyvan (2001, chapter 1) discusses the Indispensability Argument's formulation in more detail.

acceptable process of inference (which might include deduction, induction, or abduction). What exactly counts as a scientific tenet and an acceptable process of inference may not always be entirely clear. Modulo these clarifications, the version of naturalism just stated and others to be canvassed express well-defined norms.

We do not know of any contemporary biconditional naturalists, for good reason.[7] For if science does not speak to a question, or at least does not return an unequivocal answer to it, there may still be sufficiently strong evidence to believe or disbelieve a particular answer to it. Possible examples include whether God exists or what right moral action consists in.

A somewhat more modest version of naturalism is:[8]

> *Trumping Naturalism*: If science endorses *p*, one should believe *p*.

In contrast to the biconditional version, this trumping version has many supporters. For instance, Burgess and Rosen express their naturalism as follows: "The naturalists' commitment is ... to the comparatively modest proposition that when science speaks with a firm and unified voice, the philosopher is either obliged to accept its conclusions or to offer what are recognizably scientific reasons for resisting them" (1997, p. 65). Many others have upheld Trumping Naturalism, or something in its vicinity.[9]

Trumping Naturalism (or something like it) seems to animate the Indispensability Argument, specifically its first premise. If a collection of claims is part of our best present scientific theories, and omitting these claims from our theories would render the theories scientifically inferior, then we should be committed to the claims in question. There is no vantage point outside science from which to criticize the established findings of science – no "first philosophy prior to natural science," as Quine disparagingly called it.[10] So if best science indispensably uses mathematics, there can be no good reasons from outside science to reject the truth of mathematics.

Trumping Naturalism, however, is too strong a thesis. The history of science counsels that it would be foolhardy to commit ourselves to currently leading

---

[7] Perhaps Quine was one. Although Mark Colyvan's statement of one of the Indispensability Argument's premises is a version of Biconditional Naturalism, we doubt he espouses anything quite this strong. His formulation of the premise, with italics added to highlight its biconditional nature, is that "We ought to have ontological commitment to *all and only* the entities that are indispensable to our best scientific theories" (Colyvan 2019, §1).

[8] We prefer "Trumping Naturalism" to "Conditional Naturalism" for vividness.

[9] See the many references in Paseau (forthcoming a) or Daly and Liggins (2011).

[10] In, for example, Quine (1981, p. 67).

scientific theories without reservation; it suggests rather that these theories are at best only approximately true. For example, such was the success of Newtonian mechanics in the eighteenth and nineteenth centuries that it was generally deemed not just true, but definitively true. Einstein's 1905 special theory of relativity shattered this confidence. Newtonian mechanics, it is now thought, gives very close though not entirely exact predictions, so in this sense closely approximates the truth in many contexts. Yet its ontology of absolute space and time has been repudiated, so it also contains claims now regarded as outright false. Writers such as Penelope Maddy have also stressed the role of idealizations in science, which are not regarded as literally true (more on this in Section 4.1).

The situation is somewhat different with mathematics. Here the picture of strictly cumulative progress is on safer ground. That much of currently applied mathematics is true is easier to defend. Specifically in connection with the replacement of one scientific theory by another, Bangu (2012, chapter 9) points out that mathematics features in the theories of the workings of all but the most basic observation instruments (telescopes, microscopes, etc.). These instruments are used to collect the data on the basis of which it is argued that a currently held theory should be replaced by a proposed successor. So even if, as some would have it, much science is later shown to be false, the very mechanism by which that is done usually leaves intact the applied mathematics it uses. This is another challenge to the Indispensability Argument that we shall come back to.

What we have called Trumping Naturalism was, for Quine, a fundamental commitment not susceptible to further justification.[11] Others have sought to justify it directly, mostly in terms of track-record considerations. These attempted justifications observe that recent science has been very successful whereas, time and again, philosophy and other nonscientific disciplines have failed. In particular, in cases of conflict, science has a better track record than other forms of inquiry. Many philosophers sympathetic to this argument have cited approvingly David Lewis' credo to the effect that it would be absurd to reject mathematics on philosophical grounds (Lewis 1991, pp. 58–9).[12] Although Lewis' focus was on mathematics, the naturalist's sentiment extends to scientists of any stripe.

---

[11] Though Quine did not call it that, nor did he call his brand of naturalism methodological, and as noted earlier he appeared to embrace the even stronger Biconditional Naturalism.

[12] A famous example is the rejection of classical mathematics by the Dutch intuitionist L. E. J. Brouwer. One can interpret him as holding that mathematical objects are mental rather than abstract. Brouwer went on to build a radically novel mathematics on the basis of this philosophical conviction.

Critics of the track-record argument for naturalism allege that it cannot justify a form of naturalism as strong as the trumping version. Daly and Liggins (2011), who call the kind of respect for science at issue here "deferentialism," argue, against Lewis, that many philosophically motivated revisions to science-cum-mathematics would not clash with practice in any important way.[13] Moreover, they urge, track-record considerations prove too much, since they seem to "discredit the reliability of philosophical grounds for believing anything" (2011, p. 328). One of us (Paseau, forthcoming a) has also argued that a consistent naturalist should not be a dogmatist; they may accord greater weight to scientific than nonscientific considerations, but not absolute weight to the former at the expense of the latter. Moreover, as a result of the considerable disagreement in philosophy, there is no single perspective from which philosophy has a poor track record. (For example, if you are a Berkeleyan idealist you will *not* think idealism was first firmly accepted by philosophy but later discredited.)[14]

In addition to these, there is a telling criticism of simple-minded naturalist attempts to settle traditional philosophical debates, such as whether mathematical objects exist. Even if Trumping Naturalism were true, it would not be the philosophical panacea it purports to be, for there would remain difficult questions about what science endorses *all things considered*. Just because linguistics finds it convenient to assume that "Mother Teresa was a good person" is a truth-valued sentence, for example, does not mean that science does so all things considered. Whether we should regard the sentence as truth-valued based on science as a whole remains just as stubborn a question as ever, since we will have to take in much more than narrowly linguistic considerations.[15] Another way to put the point is that, since indispensability is an all-things-considered notion, it cannot be settled by a superficial look at science. The pros and cons of various interpretations of science must be carefully assessed.

To see how this last point plays out in the context of the Indispensability Argument, we note, as we did earlier, that the natural sciences make heavy use of mathematics. They appear to refer to and quantify over numbers, functions, geometric shapes and solids, sets, and the like. However, suppose that questions of mathematical ontology should ultimately be settled by scientific considerations. One might then argue that (i) the fewer types of mathematical objects posited the better, and that (ii) the principle of ontological economy

---

[13] Daly and Liggins focus on mathematics and linguistics but their point generalizes.

[14] Of course, that raises the issue of why there is more disagreement in philosophy than in science, and what this shows about philosophy's credibility. But this "disagreement" or "lack of convergence" argument is distinct from the track-record argument. For more, see Paseau (forthcoming, a).

[15] Paseau (forthcoming, a) and (2005) press versions of this point.

expressed in (i) is a tenet of scientific theory choice. Or, as mentioned earlier, one might argue that although science endorses the truth of accepted mathematics, it does not endorse the existence of mathematical objects.[16] Or, at any rate, that determining whether it does requires weighing up the pros and cons of various positions, proceeding very much in the manner of contemporary philosophy of mathematics.[17] For example, platonism may not follow even if, on the surface, accepting Maxwell's equations (fundamental to electromagnetism) commits you to abstract differential operators. Broadly scientific considerations may show that the equations' surface reading is not the correct one.

Finally, even if science does endorse an ontology of abstract objects, it may not straightforwardly endorse a particular one.[18] Would physics really be worse off, for example, if mathematical objects turned out to be categories or objects in a category rather than sets? It seems not. Although naturalism gives us a steer on these thorny debates, its mere invocation is not enough to get us out of the briar patch of philosophical(-like) controversy.

To recap, the Indispensability Argument's first premise is supported by Trumping Naturalism. Whether Trumping Naturalism can be motivated by track-record considerations remains unclear, dubious even. And even if Trumping Naturalism is true, there remains an awful lot of philosophical work to do to determine what exactly it is that science endorses.

Still, even if nothing quite as strong as Trumping Naturalism is true, most philosophers today – and that includes us – would want to give a *lot* of weight to scientific considerations. If it turns out that science cannot be done well without assuming abstract objects, that would be a strong reason to believe in abstract objects. Not an indefeasible reason, but a very strong one nonetheless. This slightly weaker version of naturalism than the trumping version supports a claim that falls only a little short of the Indispensability Argument's first premise. It supports not quite the claim that we ought rationally to be ontologically committed to scientifically indispensable objects, but rather that there are very strong rational grounds to be ontologically committed to them.

---

[16] See Paseau (2007).

[17] For example, weighing up the respective merits of platonism and eliminative structuralism. Roughly, eliminative structuralism takes any mathematical statement as a claim about what holds in any structure satisfying some axioms. For example, arithmetic is not about the natural numbers but about any structure that satisfies the axioms of arithmetic (usually taken to be the Dedekind–Peano axioms). This form of structuralism is eliminative because it does not posit any objects to back up the truth of thus-interpreted mathematical claims.

[18] See chapter 12 of Paseau (forthcoming, b).

2.2 Maddy's Second Philosophy

Penelope Maddy is probably the most influential contemporary naturalist in the philosophy of mathematics, so a quick summary of her views is in order. (This short section may be skipped without loss of continuity.) In a series of publications, most notably in her book *Second Philosophy*, Maddy (2007) has developed a form of naturalism which she calls "Second Philosophy." In a nutshell, the Second Philosopher begins with observation and experimentation and progresses from there to theory formation and testing. Improving and correcting her account of nature by this back-and-forth dialogue between observation and theory, she eventually reaches questions we could classify as philosophical. Examples include whether we can hold reliable beliefs about the external world or whether mathematical objects exist. Second Philosophy consists in the answers such a character would give to those questions. And as Maddy depicts her, the Second Philosopher lacks a principled distinction between "science" and "nonscience"; consequently, she cannot so much as state the trumping naturalist's credo.[19]

Maddy is surely right that the line between science and nonscience is not easy to draw. However, Maddy's Second Philosopher does engage with questions typically classified as philosophical, and when doing so she returns answers more or less identical to those a self-avowed trumping naturalist would. The Second Philosopher thus proceeds piecemeal, behaving much as a trumping naturalist might, but without subscribing to a global naturalist doctrine. The question is whether this refusal to embrace a global expression of her epistemic behavior is a satisfactory stance – at least for a reflective Second Philosopher. We find this question an interesting and important one but here we must put it to one side, as it does not directly affect the rest of the discussion.

2.3 Confirmational Holism

As we saw in Section 1, the Indispensability Argument stems from Quine, who subscribed to naturalism (Section 2.1). Quine also subscribed to another doctrine, which many believe props up the Indispensability Argument: confirmational holism.[20] According to it, the unit of justification is a cluster of theories rather than a single hypothesis – or, in an extreme version, the whole of science.

---

[19] The summary in this paragraph lightly paraphrases a passage in Maddy (forthcoming).

[20] Also known as justificatory or epistemological holism, and not to be confused with semantic holism (the idea that the meaning of a sentence depends on the meaning of all other sentences in the language). We use the pairs of words – such as "justificatory" and "confirmational," "justify" and "confirm" – interchangeably. An excellent account of Quine's philosophy of mathematics may be found in Resnik (2005).

Confirmational holism is sometimes known as the Duhem–Quine thesis, after Quine and Pierre Duhem.[21] The Duhem–Quine thesis has its source in the insight that scientific statements imply observational claims only in conjunction with auxiliary hypotheses. Let H and O respectively denote a hypothesis and an observation statement, and let each A_i (with index i) be an auxiliary statement. To say that observation statements entail hypotheses only in conjunction with auxiliary statements is to say that $H \& A_1 \& A_2 \& \ldots \& A_n$ entail O but that H does not do so on its own. The Duhem–Quine thesis takes this apparent fact about entailment (or scientific prediction) and flips it into a thesis about justification. An observational statement such as O justifies not H on its own but the conjunction $H \& A_1 \& A_2 \& \ldots \& A_n$. Conversely, a contrary observation does not justify the rejection of a single hypothesis H; rather, it justifies the rejection of $H \& A_1 \& A_2 \& \ldots \& A_n$, that is, at least one of $H, A_1, A_2, \ldots, A_n$. As Quine puts it:

> Suppose an experiment has yielded a result contrary to a theory currently held in some natural science. The theory comprises a whole bundle of conjoint hypotheses, or is resoluble into such a bundle. The most that the experiment shows is that at least one of these hypotheses is false; it does not show which. It is only the theory as a whole, and not any of the hypotheses, that admits of evidence or counter-evidence in observation and experiment. (Quine 1970, p. 5)

Take, for example, Sir Arthur Eddington's eclipse experiment in May 1919, designed to test which (if any) of Newtonian mechanics or Einsteinian general relativity is correct. Einstein's theory predicted that at the moment of the eclipse, light rays from stars would be deflected by twice the amount predicted by Newton's theory. There were two observation stations, one in Brazil and one in Príncipe (off the west coast of Africa). Photographs from Príncipe were dim but could, on the back of some complex calculations, be interpreted as favoring Einstein's theory. Photographs from one of the Brazilian telescopes suggested an Einsteinian shift, but photographs from the second Brazilian telescope indicated a Newtonian one. To further complicate matters, the sun's heating systematically biased both Brazilian telescopes, or so Eddington argued. In popular accounts, Eddington's expedition is often presented as a crucial experiment to cleanly test the relative merits of Newton and Einstein's theories of gravitation. But clearly it did no such thing: at best, it tested those theories combined with a host of auxiliary assumptions about telescopes' optical properties, their thermal properties, the positions of the stars, and so on.[22]

---

[21] For Duhem, see in particular his 1906/2007 work.

[22] We have drawn on the fascinating account of Eddington's experiment in chapter 2 of Strevens (2020).

The ideal gas law $PV = nRT$ illustrates the same holistic point. To test the law, one must measure the pressure (P), volume (V), and temperature (T) of a gas. (R is a constant and n is the number of moles of the gas.) Use of a thermometer to determine T presupposes a theory of how it works; ditto for the use of a barometer to measure P; and to determine the volume V of gas one must employ at least some geometry. The measurement of the number n similarly rests on chemical theory. An experimental test of an equation as simple as the gas law $PV = nRT$ thus implicitly rests on a considerable amount of "measuring theory" – a large mix of science and mathematics.

What does all this imply for mathematics? Since mathematics is used in natural science and science is empirically confirmed, mathematics is thereby also confirmed. Actually, to put it this way is a little misleading, for it would be naive to suppose that the mathematics used in science could be cleaved from the nonmathematical parts. Applied mathematics cannot be separated from science in any meaningful way, given many scientific statements' mathematical formulation. Think for example of Newton's law of gravitation relating the force between two particles to their masses and the distance between them,

$$F_g = \frac{Gm_1m_2}{r^2}.$$

So a more accurate way of putting the point would be as follows. Because empirical evidence justifies mathematics-using science, it justifies mathematics *tout court*.

Confirmational holists such as Quine do not deny that there are degrees of "empiricalness," after a fashion. A statement about a nearby object's observable properties – for example, that the table before me is brown – is obviously closer to the interface between world and theory than Fermat's Last Theorem, encountered earlier. Quine makes this point vividly in a metaphor that places mathematics and logic at the center of our total theory of the world and observational statements at its "edges": "The totality of our so-called knowledge or beliefs, from the most casual matters of geography and history to the profoundest laws of atomic physics or even of pure mathematics and logic, is a man-made fabric which impinges on experience only along the edges" (Quine 1951, p. 42).

The most famous Quinean metaphor for this idea is the "web of belief." Since the web is essentially seamless, there are no a priori statements. Everything is empirical, justified ultimately by its ability to help us make sense of experience.

Any statement can be held true come what may, if we make drastic enough adjustments elsewhere in the system. Even a statement very close to the periphery [of the web] can be held true in the face of recalcitrant experience by pleading hallucination or by amending certain statements of the kind called logical laws. Conversely, by the same token, no statement is immune to revision. Revision even of the logical law of the excluded middle has been proposed as a means of simplifying quantum mechanics; and what difference is there in principle between such a shift and the shift whereby Kepler superseded Ptolemy, or Einstein Newton, or Darwin Aristotle? (Quine 1951, p. 43)

One question that immediately springs to mind is what a confirmational holist such as Quine should say about unapplied mathematics. Many mathematical theorems have yet to find empirical application. So is an unapplied theorem of, say, arithmetic unjustified? No, says Quine. Because the axioms of arithmetic have been confirmed by scientific application, so have its resulting theorems, be they applied or unapplied or even inapplicable. Schematically (where " $\dots$ $\overset{j}{\to} \dots$ " abbreviates "justifies"):

Empirical Evidence $\overset{j}{\to}$ Mathematics used in science $\overset{j}{\to}$ Axioms $\overset{j}{\to}$ Theorems

In this section, we set out a version of (methodological) naturalism as well as confirmational holism (and briefly mentioned Maddy's Second Philosophy). How do naturalism and holism combine to support the Indispensability Argument's first premise? According to naturalism, we should be committed to our best scientific theories. By confirmational holism, commitment to our best scientific theories brings with it ontological commitment to the entities that feature in their indispensable parts – colloquially, their "moving parts." Putting the two together yields the Indispensability Argument's first premise: we ought to be ontologically committed to objects that are indispensable to our best scientific theories.[23]

To preview the discussion in Section 4, there is, however, a potential clash between naturalism and confirmational holism, noted by Maddy. Roughly, naturalism tells you to take scientific practice seriously, and confirmational holism tells you to believe in all the entities invoked by scientists. What if the two are in conflict? What if scientific practice is not in fact committed to some of the entities routinely invoked in science? We shall examine this possibility in more detail in Section 4.

A related point is that confirmational holism is, on the face of it, an overly strong thesis. Suppose that hypothesis H and auxiliary claims $A_1, \dots, A_n$ entail O (but H does not entail O on its own). Then $H, A_1, \dots, A_n$ and a random claim

---

[23] As we saw in Section 2.1, that premise needs to be weakened if any acceptable naturalism falls short of the trumping version. We will henceforth take this sort of qualification as read.

C that has been tacked on to this list *also* imply *O*.[24] So if facts about implication can be automatically flipped into facts about justification, *C* would be confirmed by the observation of *O*, alongside *H* and $A_1, \ldots, A_n$. But *C* was any old claim; it may have nothing to do with *O* and could just as well have been not-*C*. Surely something has gone wrong here: observing *O* does not confirm *C*. This problem is well-known to confirmation theory.[25]

In response, indispensabilists should concede that a strong version of confirmational holism is untenable. Hypotheses that are not "pulling their weight" in such an implication or in explanation are not confirmed. But indispensabilists will insist that hypotheses that are pulling their weight – as the "moving parts" – *are* confirmed. And they will add that mathematics plays this sort of role in many scientific explanations. How to cash out the metaphors of pulling one's weight or being a moving part may be difficult. But it is not clear that the indispensabilist is under an obligation to spell this out in detail, so long as it is reasonably plausible that mathematics does pull its weight in scientific explanation and is a moving part, unlike the tacked-on claim *C*. In other words, the first premise of the Indispensability Argument may be plausible even if a strong version of confirmational holism is not. The word "indispensable," which gives the overall argument its name, really is crucial. Critics of the argument will now question whether mathematics does in fact play such an indispensable role. We will detail their views in the coming sections.

To sum up our progress so far. We introduced the Indispensability Argument (Section 1) and motivated its first premise, via the combination of naturalism (Section 2.1) and confirmational holism (Section 2.3). We noted some issues with naturalism and, by way of preview, with confirmational holism as well. We now turn to the argument's second premise, that mathematical objects are indispensable to our best scientific theories. As we now move beyond the statement of the Indispensability Argument and its motivation, we shift from more expository to more critical discussion.

3 Hard Road Nominalism: Field's Program

In Section 2, we focused on the Indispensability Argument's first premise. We now switch gears and turn our attention to its second premise.

3.1 Outline

The second premise's most influential opponent is Hartry Field. Field is a *nominalist*: he denies the existence of abstract mathematical objects. Field's 1980 manifesto, *Science Without Numbers*, which made waves in philosophy, is

---

[24] Adding *C* to a premise set cannot turn a logical implication into a nonimplication.

[25] For a helpful summary, see Morrison (2010).

a defense of nominalism against the Indispensability Argument. As mentioned in Section 1, he sees this argument as the only non-question-begging one for the truth of mathematics.

Field objects to the argument's second premise because he thinks mathematical objects are not indispensable to our best scientific theories. Put informally, he thinks science can make do without mathematical objects. The reason, roughly, is that mathematics is *conservative* – it does not help us establish anything about the physical world that could not be established without it. As he puts it:

> if we take a mathematical theory that includes bridge laws (i.e. includes assertions of the existence of functions from physical objects into "pure" abstract objects, including perhaps assertions obtained via a comprehension principle that uses mathematical and physical vocabulary in the same breath), then that mathematics is applicable to the world, i.e. it is useful in enabling us to draw nominalistically-statable conclusions from nominalistically-statable premises; *but here, unlike in the case of physics, the conclusions we arrive at by these means are not genuinely new, they are already derivable in a more long-winded fashion from the premises, without recourse to the mathematical entities.* (Field 1980, pp. 10–11, italics in the original)

Lightly symbolized, the idea is that the mathematical portion, M^T, of any scientific theory, T, is conservative over T's nominalization, N^T. That is to say, no N^T-expressible claims follow from the combination of M^T and N^T that do not follow from N^T on its own.[26] And for Field, nominalized scientific theories (N^T) are at least as good as their usual mathematics-using counterparts. Since by definition these nominalized theories do not refer to or quantify over mathematical objects, mathematical objects are a *dispensable* part of best science: it *can* manage without them. And because for Field there is no other reason to suppose generally accepted mathematical statements are true, he duly rejects their truth.[27]

Since the nominalization of all science would be an immense undertaking, Field contents himself with illustrating his nominalistic strategy. To give the reader a flavor of what this involves, we briefly review Field's nominalization of space-time. Suppose that *ST* is a domain of space-time points. The primitives on *ST* may be taken as:

a 3-place predicate $Bet(x, y, z)$ ('y is between x and z')

a 4-place predicate $Cong(x, y, z, w)$ ("the line from x to y is congruent to that between z and w")

---

[26] There is a technical issue here over what "follow from" means, which we will skate over.

[27] With a caveat about universal statements (e.g. "all groups have an inverse element") which are vacuously true, in this instance because there are no groups.

The notion of a point being between two others, so that the point lies on the line segment joining the other two, is clear enough. Intuitively, two line segments are congruent if and only if they are of the same length. Using these, and derivative notions defined in an appropriate logic, one may axiomatize *ST* in such a way that its only models are isomorphic to $\mathbb{R}^4$ (four-dimensional euclidean space).

To carry out classical physics, in which one of the coordinates is time and the other three are spatial, we also need two further primitives:

a 2-place predicate $Simul(x, y)$ ('x is simultaneous with y')

a 4-place spatial congruence predicate $S\text{-}Cong(x, y, z, w)$ (which holds if x is simultaneous to y, z is simultaneous to w, and the spatial distances from x to y and from z to w are congruent)

Note that Field admits space-time regions and points.[28] Space-time points, which are space-time regions of minimal size, are concrete because they are part of – indeed constitute – space-time itself. His own nominalization of the differential fragment of Newtonian gravitational theory – his illustration of a scientific theory in *Science Without Numbers* – is formulated in a second-order language, whose first-order variables range over space-time points, and whose second-order variables range over regions of space-time points. To avoid commitment to sets, Field takes these regions to be mereological sums/fusions of space-time points. So membership of a point in a region is, for him, not a set-theoretic but a mereological relation. And containment of a subregion in a region is not (set-theoretic) subsethood but mereological inclusion. Field believes that mereology is nominalistically kosher, because by his lights it does not appeal to mathematical entities. The mereological sum of my body parts, for example, is my body, which is a physical entity, not a mathematical one.

Axiomatizing space-time using these primitives enables us to prove a representation theorem along these lines:

A structure $<A, \text{Bet}_A, \text{Simul}_A, \text{S-Cong}_A>$ is a model of the axioms iff there is a one-one function ϕ from A onto $\mathbb{R}^4$, with respective projections to the first to fourth coordinates, $\phi_1, \phi_2, \phi_3, \phi_4$, such that if we define the (euclidean) distance function $d_\phi(x, y) \leq$ for x, y in A as

$$d_\phi(x, y) = \left(\sum_{1 \leq i \leq 4}(\phi_i(x) - \phi_i(y))^2\right)^{1/2}$$

then

---

[28] He notes that only "fairly regular" regions are required for his purposes (Field 1980, p. 37). Many philosophers have queried whether space-time points are nominalistically acceptable entities.

(i) $\forall x \forall y [Bet(x,y,z) \leftrightarrow d_\phi(x,y) + d_\phi(y,z) = d_\phi(x,z)]$

(ii) $\forall x \forall y [Simul(x,y) \leftrightarrow \phi_4(x) = \phi_4(y)]$

(iii) $\forall x \forall y [S - Cong(x,y,z,w) \leftrightarrow \phi_4(x) = \phi_4(y) \land \phi_4(z) = \phi_4(w) \land d_\phi(x,y)$
$= d_\phi(z,w)]$

The only primitive spatiotemporal predicates needed to describe Newtonian space-time are those in this axiom system; all others are defined in terms of them. Informally, the idea is that we use the axioms to characterize a four-dimensional isomorphic image of $\mathbb{R}^4$ using nominalistically acceptable language. The representation theorem allows us to derive conclusions about spatiotemporal betweenness, simultaneity, and spatial congruence without reference to mathematical objects.

Field goes on to discuss theories about physical processes in a space-time of this type. Though the details are more complicated, the basic idea is the same. The aim is to nominalize the contents of the theory by using conditions that pin down the relevant mathematical structure. Success is achieved just when appropriate representation theorems can be proved (in a set theory external to the theories in question).

Returning to Field's overall strategy, one way to think of the argument is as a *reductio ad absurdum* of the hypothesis that mathematical objects exist. Because establishing his conservativeness claim involves the use of mathematics, Field may be said to be using standard mathematics against itself. As he puts it, "platonism is left in an unstable position: it entails its own unjustifiability" (Field 1980, p. 6).[29]

Because Field's opposition to the Indispensability Argument's second premise involves arduous reconstruction of scientific theories, it has come to be known as "Hard Road Nominalism." Many nominalists believe, however, that it is impossible to formulate nominalistic theories à la Field. They spurn Field's sedulous reconstructions, preferring instead Easy Road Nominalism, whose success does not rest on nominalizing science.[30]

To introduce this alternative to Field's approach, we note that Field, like Quine, is a self-avowed naturalist. As such, he wants his theory to be not only spatiotemporally adequate but also scientifically attractive. Indeed, at the start of *Science Without Numbers*, he avows an interest in only "reasonably attractive" alternative theories (Field 1980, p. 8), and reiterates this later on (Field 1980, pp. 41, 47). The right theory must be the overall simplest one (1980, p. 97). In particular, one important dimension of a scientific theory's

---

[29] Field believes that the nominalist can also trust the argument for conservativeness, despite its use of mathematics (1980, p. 14 fn. 10).

[30] In the preface to the 2016 revised edition of *Science Without Numbers*, Field expresses a surprising amount of sympathy for the Easy Road approach. The "Easy Road" terminology is owed to Colyvan (2010).

attractiveness is its explanatoriness. How explanatory a theory is therefore has a significant effect on the extent to which it is "reasonably attractive."

This is where Easy Road Nominalism comes in. According to it, our usual (mathematics-exploiting) scientific theories are explanatory only by virtue of underlying physical – and not mathematical – entities, properties, and relationships. Although scientific theories avail themselves of mathematics to represent these entities, properties, and relationships, the real explanatory work is done not by the mathematics but by the physical structures themselves. Or, for a slightly different version of Easy Road Nominalism, mathematical theories do play an indispensable explanatory role in providing structural explanations of physical phenomena. But given the form of these explanations, they require no mathematical entities, only the approximate instantiation of mathematical structures in physical systems.[31]

So which "road" should the nominalist take? Field's Hard Road, or later nominalists' easier path? This is a question that will occupy us in later sections once we have seen some of the issues the Hard Road faces.

3.2 Objections

The literature on Field's program and its ramifications is vast and still growing. In this Element, we cannot pretend to do it justice. We do, however, survey some of the key objections to it. Echoing others in the literature, we take these objections to show that Field has not undermined the Indispensability Argument's second premise.

A first objection is that Field has not produced nominalizations of more complex physical theories. His critics allege that there is no available nominalization of theories such as quantum mechanics in which the objects represented by the mathematics are not themselves concrete. A state vector in the Hilbert-space formulation is not the sort of thing that can form the basis for a nominalization project, because the nominalistically unacceptable mathematics that is doing the representing, while replaceable, is only replaceable in terms of something equally nominalistically unsatisfactory (propositions or eventualities). David Malament was perhaps the first to raise the objection in print:

> Quantum mechanics is even a more recalcitrant example than Hamiltonian mechanics. Here I do not really see how Field can get started at all. I suppose one can think of the theory as determining a set of models – each a Hilbert space. But what form would the recovery (i.e., representation) theorem take? The only possibility that comes to mind is a theorem of the sort sought by

---

[31] For this second version, see Leng (2021). The position outlined there seems to have merged into the modal-structuralist account of applications (for modal-structuralism, see Hellman 1989).

Jauch, Piron, *et al.* They start with "propositions" (or "eventualities") and lattice-theoretic relations as primitive, and then seek to prove that the lattice of propositions is necessarily isomorphic to the lattice of subspaces of some Hilbert space. But of course no theorem of this sort would be of any use to Field. What could be worse than propositions (or eventualities)? (Malament 1982, pp. 533–4)

Malament adds that quantum-mechanical field theories provide further examples. In general, theories formulated in terms of phase spaces are not likely to be susceptible to Field's nominalization strategy. In these cases, the mathematical objects present a range of physical possibilities that go beyond what is physically realized. Physical reality itself corresponds indirectly to mathematical features of these state spaces; at best, parts of it are isomorphic to substructures within these spaces.

The nominalist may retort that the difficulty stems from our deficient understanding of quantum mechanics. When it comes to the interpretation of quantum mechanics – what quantum mechanics is about – we see through a glass, darkly. Though candidate interpretations abound, each of them is beset with difficulties, and none has achieved consensus among experts. Only when we can separate what it says about the physical world from its mathematical machinery will we understand quantum mechanics properly, nominalists might urge. Or to put it another way, only when we are able to nominalize it.

Although we sympathize with this line of thought, it leaves nominalism hostage to scientific fortune. Field's insistence that scientific theories are cleanly separable into a nominalistic part and a mathematical part may turn out to be based on an outmoded, pre-twentieth-century conception of a scientific theory. At the start of the twenty-first century, it remains at best unclear whether we will ever be able to nominalize all scientific theories, in particular quantum theory and other parts of mathematical physics that make heavy use of phase spaces. Overall, there is reason to suppose that Field's program will be defeated by more advanced theories.[32] Indeed, Field's own preface to the second edition of *Science Without Numbers* (Field 2016) sounds a pessimistic note on this front.

A second problem for Field is that the nominalization program is likely to be piecemeal. If, as appears to be case, there is no standard procedure for nominalization,[33] the nominalistic total theory of everything, N^{TT} (*TT* standing for "total theory"), is made up of a miscellany of theories, $N_1^T, N_2^T, \ldots$. These nominalistic theories of space-time, Newtonian mechanics, physical chemistry, fluid mechanics, and so on have little in common, save their nominalistic

---

[32] For further discussion, see Malament's (1982) review of *Science Without Numbers*, Meyer (2009), Putnam (2012, pp. 191–2), and Urquhart (1990), .

[33] As Field concedes (2016, p. P–20).

credentials. This compares unfavorably to standard, mathematics-involving theories. The mathematics common to all of them lends them much of their unity, which is why they are collectively simpler. The fact that T_1, T_2, ..., all use the same mathematics greatly unifies and simplifies science. Burgess and Rosen (1997) more generally argue that nominalistic scientific theories are inferior, by the usual scientific standards, than (the usual) platonist ones. Field has privileged ontological economy, as well as intrinsicness of explanation,[34] at the expense of a host of other scientific virtues.[35] So even if mathematics is conservative over nominalized science, that does not mean that it is scientifically dispensable.

A third and final problem in a by-no-means exhaustive list is based on the distinction between mathematical nominalism – the claim that abstract mathematical entities do not exist – and global nominalism, the claim that no abstract objects exist.[36] The question is whether one can be a mathematical nominalist but not a global nominalist. If not, what does that say about mathematical nominalism?

To take the first question first, notice that the argument in *Science Without Numbers* is negative. Field does not offer positive support for nominalism (Field 1980, p. 4; Field 2016, p. P–1). His aim, rather, is to defend nominalism from platonistic attack and thereby defeat the only serious argument for platonism (as he sees it). In principle, you could proceed similarly in other domains: you could be a piecemeal global nominalist by rejecting each type of abstract object for piecemeal reasons. For example, you might argue that abstract mathematical objects do not exist for reason R_1, that abstract concepts do not exist for reason R_2, that abstract properties and relations do not exist for reason R_3, that abstract propositions do not exist for reason R_4, and so on. But in practice global nominalism is never piecemeal: global nominalists reject the existence of all abstract objects *on account of their abstractness*. It is part and parcel of nominalism as usually conceived that the existence of abstract entities should be rejected for this general reason.

We illustrate this point with two examples. One motivation for mathematical nominalism is epistemological: we should not posit abstract mathematical objects because we cannot have justifiable/warranted/grounded/reliable beliefs about them,[37] as they are not causally connected to us. This issue is sometimes

---

[34] Field claims that underlying every good extrinsic explanation there is an intrinsic explanation. An intrinsic explanation explains the physical facts without appeal to extraneous entities, such as numbers, that play no causal role in the given situation. As Field sees it, both nominalists and platonists should prefer intrinsic explanations or laws to extrinsic ones (1980, p. 43).

[35] Including perhaps also heuristic power, as argued in chapter 5 of Bangu (2012).

[36] "Agnostic" versions of both claims (as opposed to "atheist" ones) could similarly be distinguished.

[37] The list of adjectives is to allow for different epistemological variants.

known as the "access problem" for platonism. Field espouses this sort of motivation in work following the publication of *Science Without Numbers* Field (1989, pp. 25–30).[38] Piecemeal nominalism is therefore unattractive: if motivated in this way, it must apply across the board if it applies anywhere. Some alleged nominalists make an exception for things like linguistic types (such as the letter "A," over and above any of its tokens), which you might suppose we can access via their tokens. But how precisely do we "access" these types? It cannot be causally, since types are abstract. And if it is by inference from tokens that we observe (e.g. the occurrences of "A" on this page or screen), why is that route not also open to us in at least some mathematical cases? Why can we not in the same way access geometrical triangles or squares instantiated or approximated by physical ones, or the cyclic group of order 4 via its physical instantiations (consider for example a jerky wheel that you can rotate by 90°), or mathematical graphs via physical networks, and so on?

Another motivation for nominalism is ontological economy. It would be best to avoid commitment to mathematical abstract objects, if possible. But this motivation obviously generalizes: avoiding commitment to *all* abstract objects would obviously be an even greater boon. It would promote both qualitative ontological economy (by avoiding commitment to all types of abstract objects and hence to the general type *abstract object*) and quantitative ontological economy (by avoiding commitment to many other abstract objects).

Our discussion, though brief, suggests that mathematical nominalism leads to global nominalism. In any case, mathematical nominalists tend to be global nominalists. You would be hard pushed to find a philosopher wary of abstract mathematical objects but at the same time perfectly happy to countenance other sorts of abstracta.[39]

Global nominalism, however, is untenable, for two principal reasons. One is that talk of abstract objects is pervasive. Abstract types, for example, occur in all branches of science as well as in everyday language. The first chapter of Linda Wetzel's book on types and tokens (Wetzel 2009) takes randomly chosen passages of scientific and nonscientific text and italicizes occurrences of terms referring to types to show how prevalent type talk – and therefore talk of abstract objects – is. Consider for instance the following list of types:

> species, genes, epigenotypes, languages, body parts like the larynx, syllables,
> vowels,allophones, computers like the Altair 8800, Mozart's Coronation

---

[38] It is in this collection more generally that Field summarizes the positive motivation for nominalism missing from *Science Without Numbers*.

[39] The reverse combination of views – nominalism about everything but mathematical objects – is more natural and was instantiated, as we read him, by Quine. In his mature philosophy, he was a reluctant platonist about mathematics and a nominalist about everything else.

Concerto, the Queen's gambit, the hydrogen atom, the football and so on.
(Wetzel 2009, p. 23)

If we are to avoid reference to abstract objects, we must do so across all areas of discourse, which are awash with references to abstract objects. Yet Field has not given us a recipe that generalizes beyond mathematics. Nor has anyone else ever articulated a plausible nominalist reconstrual of *all* discourse, mathematical as well as nonmathematical. Chapters 3 and 4 of Wetzel (2009) contain strong arguments against attempts to do so – so-called paraphrase strategies (paraphrasing abstract-object talk in terms of concrete objects). Of course, some of this discourse may not be scientific in any strict sense, and so a naturalist may choose to ignore it; but as many of the examples in Wetzel's list demonstrate, at least a good deal of it is.

The second problem for global nominalism is that mathematical nominalists must invoke abstract objects in order to articulate their nominalism. In particular, Field, in defending his nominalism, refers to theories, for example specific mathematical theories such as Zermelo-Fraenkel set theory with Choice (ZFC), or nominalist scientific theories. But what *are* theories? What, for instance, is ZFC set theory? A platonist has a ready answer: the abstract set of sentence types (or propositions) of the ZFC axioms and their consequences. What, though, can the global nominalist's answer to the same question be, since by definition they set their face against all abstract objects, including sentence types and propositions?[40] Presumably, for the global nominalist, ZFC must be a collection of sentence tokens. But for most theorems p provable from ZFC, even relatively simple ones, there are no actual inscriptions or utterances of the entire proof – no actual tokenings. So a global nominalist should not believe in these proofs.

In sum, mathematical nominalists are typically global nominalists. It seems hard in principle to justify the former in a way that does not lead to the latter. But global nominalism is untenable. No one has ever managed to explain how to nominalistically reformulate even a fraction of our beliefs. A nominalist could high-handedly retort: so much the worse for most of our beliefs! But to decimate most of what we believe in order to accommodate theoretical qualms about abstract entities is unreasonable; it is no way to do philosophy. Even worse, mathematical nominalism à la Field construes theories as abstract objects. It thereby undercuts global nominalism.

---

[40] Field himself chides another would-be nominalist, Charles Chihara, for accepting uninstantiated linguistic types: "the linguistic entities that Chihara appeals to include sentence types no token of which has even been uttered, and it is not at all obvious to me whether these should count as nominalistically legitimate" (Field 1980, p. 45).

We have seen why the prospects for nominalism are bleak: science may not be nominalizable across the board; nominalist versions of scientific theories are inferior to the usual ones; and nominalism about mathematics leads to global nominalism, which is untenable. For these reasons and others, by the turn of the millennium, 20 years after the publication of *Science Without Numbers*, Field's program, though much admired for its technical prowess and philosophical ingenuity, was widely believed to have failed.

We conclude that the Indispensability Argument's second premise is relatively safe from Field's assault on it. We now examine another line of attack on the argument, which can be seen as targeting its first premise. Following it, we return to the question of Hard vs. Easy Road Nominalism.

4 An Objection from Scientific Practice

The Indispensability Argument's first premise states that we ought to be ontologically committed to objects indispensable to our best scientific theories. We saw earlier, in Section 2.1, that this premise needs to be modified, because it rests on an implausibly strong version of naturalism. Consider that done. The issue now is whether this premise really does follow from the right holistic picture of scientific confirmation (in combination with the appropriate form of naturalism). More specifically: is the first premise consonant with the practice of science itself?

4.1 A Case Study

To answer this question, we must take a closer look at science and its history. Atomic theory in the second half of the nineteenth century provides an interesting case study, developed by Penelope Maddy.[41] Modern atomic theory dates from the early 1800s, when John Dalton hypothesized that each element consists of atoms of a single type. The atomic theory was used to explain why elements react in ratios of small whole numbers, and to predict and explain chemical compounds' properties in terms of their collections of atoms. By about 1860, the atomic theory had proved so successful that it had become indispensable to science, Maddy claims. Yet in spite of all the evidence in its favor, it was still viewed with suspicion, because the evidence for the atomic theory, although extensive, remained fairly indirect. In particular, the theory had yet to be verified by direct experiment. That all changed at the start of the twentieth century, following Einstein's mathematical analysis of Brownian motion in 1905. This spurred the French physicist Jean Baptiste Perrin to perform

---

[41] Chapter II.6 of Maddy (1997).

experiments to determine the mass and dimensions of atoms. Perrin's experiments in the period 1908–13 produced direct evidence for the existence of atoms. The experiments' success led to the widespread acceptance of atomism. Maddy concludes from this episode that the indispensability and empirical success of a scientific theory are insufficient for scientists to literally believe it.

Suppose we apply the moral of this episode in the history of science to the mathematical case. If we apply scientific standards consistently across the board, we should not regard mathematics as true or scientifically confirmed simply because of its indispensability to science. Just as the scientific indispensability of late-nineteenth-century atomic theory was insufficient reason to regard it as true, so we should not take the current indispensability of mathematics as sufficient grounds for its truth.

We have cast Maddy's analogy between science and mathematics as an argument, whose conclusion may more succinctly be stated by saying that naturalism and confirmational holism are in tension. Naturalism urges a high regard for scientific methodology. In particular, it bids us respect a distinction science draws between assumptions we ought to believe and assumptions whose presence can be explained by reasons other than their literal truth. If we accept Maddy's analogy, confirmational holism is therefore too strong. Giving due regard to science entails *not* seeing all the useful parts of a scientific theory as true.[42] This, of course, is a direct challenge to the Indispensability Argument's first premise.

In response, one might point out that only five decades separated the atomic theory's first striking successes and its quasi-universal acceptance. That is hardly a huge time lag given that, as a rule, community-wide acceptance lags behind experimental confirmation. To draw upon mathematical examples from the same century, four decades separated the development of non-euclidean geometry in the late 1820s and its embrace by mainstream mathematicians in the 1860s. Group theory first got going in the period 1826–31, but did not enter the mathematical mainstream until the 1870s. Many other examples could be cited of scientific theories which took decades to be accepted. Moreover, the speed of information transmission in the second half of the nineteenth century was considerably slower than it is today. That is surely one reason why scientists were slow to be won over by atomism.

Another reason, as pertinent today as it was in the nineteenth century, is that scientific change often requires generational change. A new theory goes against the vested interests of a scientific field's "gatekeepers" – the professoriate, members of funding bodies, and so on – who can hold on to their positions

---

[42] Compare Maddy (1992, p. 281).

for decades. Senior scientists are less able, less willing, or both, to embrace revolutionary advances; their scientific worldviews are too set. As Max Planck drolly put it, science advances one funeral at a time.[43]

There are sociological reasons, then, for why scientists were slow to accept atomic theory from the 1860s on. But set these aside. Even if we ignore the sociological dimension, Maddy's case study only threatens indispensabilist platonism on a further assumption. For the moral of her case study is that a naturalist should accept a scientific theory not only when (a) the theory is indispensable to science but also when (b) the theory is believed literally by the scientific community. Mathematics meets criterion (a), claim proponents of the Indispensability Argument. If it also meets criterion (b), Maddy's point does not threaten the argument. It simply calls for a friendly amendment to its first premise: we ought to be ontologically committed to objects indispensable to our best scientific theories on condition that scientists literally believe they exist. So the crux is whether scientists tend to believe mathematics *literally*. The analogy with late-nineteenth-century atomic theory, prior to Einstein's analysis and Perrin's experiments in the early twentieth century, only holds if scientists do not do so.

4.2 Do Scientists Literally Believe Mathematics?

So: do scientists believe the mathematics used in science literally?[44] At first pass, the answer seems to be yes, and not just a guarded but a resounding yes. If you listen to what scientists say and read what they write, they seem to rely greatly on mathematics and to accept it literally. It would be very odd to come away from a physics seminar or a high-school chemistry class with the impression that the speaker or teacher did not literally believe the mathematics they made use of. The case seems to be open and shut.

But not everyone sees it that way. Following Maddy (1997, pp. 143–6), philosophers such as Mary Leng have put the focus on idealizations routinely deployed in science. In another analogy, Leng likens mathematics to these idealizations, which appear throughout science but are not literally believed. Examples include the following: the hypothesis that fluids are continuous substances; that temperature can be defined at a single spatial point (as opposed to a region); that agents are fully rational utility maximizers; or that bodies in motion encounter no air resistance.[45] Leng argues that the use of such

---

[43] This is the usual rendering of Planck's not quite so pithy statement (Planck 1950, pp. 33–4, 97), though in fairness we should note that Maddy's case study involves Poincaré and Ostwald changing their minds about the existence of atoms; no funerals were involved in either case.

[44] The discussion in Section 4.2 overlaps significantly with that in Paseau (2012).

[45] The examples are derived from Leng (2010, p. 11). She writes: "Given that the *truth* of such idealized theoretical hypotheses is not confirmed by our theoretical successes in these cases,

idealizations is not always eliminable. For instance, a Weierstrassian limit strategy cannot make sense of fluid dynamics' continuity assumption (meaning, roughly, that treating quantities as continuous does not give the same results as taking them to be limit cases of discrete quantities). This sort of ineliminability point has been challenged in the literature,[46] but let us grant it here for the sake of argument. So: if the ineliminability of a hypothesis does not entail its confirmation, should the same moral not apply to mathematics? Might mathematics not also be considered a sort of idealization, not to be taken literally? Could it be akin to the hypothesis that fluids are continuous, or that temperature is defined at a single point?

The objection before us is that we should not be committed to parts of science – understood broadly, to include the natural, social, and informational sciences – not literally believed by scientists. And, the objection continues, mathematics is one such example, so we should not, after all, be committed to all the mathematical objects posited by our best scientific theories. In other words, the Indispensability Argument's first premise is false.

To assess this point, it is useful to have a detailed and methodologically self-conscious example to work with. So let us examine the social science most closely associated with unrealistic idealizations: economics. *Macroeconomics* by Oliver Blanchard (2002) is a popular undergraduate textbook, written by a distinguished economist, which has gone through several editions. In chapter 3 of this book, Blanchard decomposes a country's gross domestic product (GDP) as

$$C + I + G + X - IM$$

where C is consumption, I is investment, G is government spending, X is exports and IM imports. Blanchard warns the reader that in thinking about the determinants of GDP "a number of simplifications" will be made. First off, we must "[a]ssume that all firms produce the same good, which can be used by consumers for consumption, by firms for investment, or by the government. With this (big) simplification, we need to look at only one market – the market for

---

then, as Maddy has pointed out, if the *mathematical* assumptions of our theories are made in the context of such literally false idealizations, we should be wary of supposing that the truth of *those* assumptions is confirmed by our theoretical successes. If all that is confirmed is that fluid dynamics has got *something* right about the nature of real fluids, why should we assume that the assumptions it makes about the nature of mathematical objects are among the assumptions that are actually confirmed as true by our theoretical successes?" (Leng 2010, p. 112). Professing a background naturalism (Leng 2010, p. 44) she adds: "Trusting science to tell us what there is should not require us to believe in all of the objects posited by our successful scientific theories, if scientists themselves think that there are good reasons to remain agnostic, or even to doubt, some of their theoretical assumptions" (Leng 2010, pp. 125–6).

[46] See for example Bangu (2012, pp. 186–91), who draws on an example from statistical mechanics.

'the' good." Next, "[a]ssume that firms are willing to supply any amount of the good at a given price, P." This assumption is a pro tem idealization: "As we shall see later in the book, this assumption is valid only in the short run. When we move to the study of the medium run (starting in Section 6), we shall need to give it up. But for the moment, the assumption will simplify our life." Furthermore, "[a]ssume that the economy is *closed*, that it does not trade with the rest of the world: Both exports and imports are zero." We are reminded that "[t]his assumption clearly goes against the facts: Modern economies trade with the rest of the world. Later on (starting in Chapter 18), we shall abandon this assumption and look at what happens when the economy is open. But, for the moment, this assumption will also simplify our life." Finally, to drill the point home, the margin contains a methodological warning for the neophyte economist: "A model nearly always starts with the word *Assume* or (*Suppose*). This is an indication that reality is about to be simplified to focus on the issue at hand."[47]

Shortly afterwards, a similar assumption is made, this time not about which variables are relevant to determining GDP, but about their relationship. Blanchard points out that "[i]t is often useful to be more specific about the form of the function. Here is such a case. It is reasonable to assume that the relation between consumption and disposable income is ... a linear relation" (Blanchard 2002, p. 49). Next, we are informed that the model will take investment as exogenous (i.e. as given – not explained by the model), "to keep our model simple. But the assumption is not innocuous." He then adds: "It is not hard to see that this implication may be a bad description of reality ... We leave this mechanism out of the model for the moment; we shall introduce a more realistic treatment of investment in Chapter 5" (Blanchard 2002, p. 50).

We have quoted Blanchard's textbook at length for a reason: to demonstrate the care and caution taken by a sophisticated model builder to highlight which of the model's assumptions are realistic and which are simplifications or idealizations. There is nothing idiosyncratic about Blanchard's attitude. Any careful model builder would do the same, although they might be less explicit about it in less pedagogical contexts.

When it comes to mathematics, however, the contrast could not be greater. The otherwise cautious, methodologically self-conscious, Blanchard turns dogmatic. A mathematical appendix presents the mathematical results used in this textbook in the usual "Definition-Proposition-Proof" form. Readers are instructed on the mathematical explanations or predictions needed to understand the models. These results are all assumed to be true and, when precisely

---

[47] Quotations in this paragraph are from Blanchard (2002, p. 48).

stated, to require no caveats. When presenting a mathematical result, Blanchard uses "know" in this connection, never "assume" or "suppose." We are never told, for example, that the geometric series (with $c \neq 1$)

$$1 + c + c^2 + \ldots + c^n$$

sums to

$$(1 - c^{n+1})/(1 - c)$$

only on condition that the series exists, or on the assumption that mathematics is true. Blanchard asserts the mathematics outright, without fuss or caution. By all appearances, he believes mathematics to be true, in contrast to the many idealizations he builds into his model of the economy. Suppose Blanchard genuinely believed mathematics was no more than a useful tool with which to derive results. That is, suppose he saw it as analogous to believed-to-be-false or at least not-believed-to-be-true assumptions, such as that imports and exports can for certain purposes be ignored, or that consumption is linear, or that investment is exogenous. Would he not, in that case, have issued one more methodological disclaimer to add to his many previous ones?

Such examples are easily multiplied. In light of them, you would expect critics of the Indispensability Argument's first premise to provide many examples of the opposite tendency. You would imagine their critique to be supported by a plethora of quotations from scientists professing agnosticism or doubts about the truth of mathematics. But not so. And the reason is clear: scientists who question mainstream mathematics are few and far between. Mary Leng cites the physicist Chris Isham, who argues that there is no a priori reason why the empirical world should be modeled using real numbers, a model that is "more than a little odd" in the context of quantum field theory. She also mentions in the same breath Richard Feynman's suspicions that geometry as we know it might not extend to infinitely small space.[48]

These are slim pickings. Moreover, the tone of the passages from which Leng quotes is also very guarded. As we have seen, Blanchard is forthright about what he sees as unrealistic assumptions in his macroeconomic model. In contrast, Isham and Feynman are more hedged, cautious, speculative – philosophical, one might say.[49] More importantly, Isham and Feynman are not questioning all the mathematics assumed in physics but only part of it – the

---

[48] For both, see Leng (2010, p. 72).

[49] Perhaps also relevant is the fact that Isham and Feynman are both writing for the layperson. Isham's article is a popular exposition of quantum gravity, while Feynman's book is based on a series of general lectures at Cornell. If the primary data of the philosophy of science is science itself, these writings are not evidently part of that data.

hypothesis that space-time is a real manifold – used in a single application. Swaths of mathematics are left untouched, including many other uses of the continuum in science, for example the use of random variables in applications of probability or the use of Hilbert spaces in quantum theory. It is hardly straightforward to "discretize" space-time, that is, base it on some countable set such as, say, Z^n or Q^n or A^n.[50] Irrational numbers such as $\sqrt{2}$ and transcendental numbers such as π or e seem essential to science, as witnessed by their countless scientific applications. The classical theory of the continuum gives a compelling general account of the numbers required for science and implies the existence of many other numbers.

The most reasonable interpretation of what Isham and Feynman are up to, then, is that they are questioning the suitability of the relevant mathematics for the job at hand rather than its truth. Moreover, they are *not* suggesting that the hypothesis that space-time is a real manifold might be supplanted by a nonmathematical characterization of reality. Any rival to the real numbers in this context is presumed to be a *mathematical* rival.

Leng, as we have seen, is a proponent of this objection to the Indispensability Argument – the "idealization" variant of Maddy's objection from scientific practice. She is aware of the fact that she is gainsaying scientists, even if she understandably wishes to play it down (Leng 2010 p. 144, p. 180). How, on her view, might we explain the discrepancy between what scientists implicitly take the role of mathematics to be and the role it allegedly plays? It looks distinctly difficult. It is hardly plausible that scientists have failed to appreciate that their use of mathematics is noncommittal. Scientists are reflective beings, who, through instinct and professional training alike, question their own assumptions as well as each other's. Yet the truth of mainstream mathematics is generally thought a safe enough assumption. When it comes to mathematics, the need for scientific circumspection is greatly diminished, even otiose. If the truth of mathematics were scientifically suspect, would scientists not have noticed?

Perhaps scientists have omitted to apply their own methods to the question of whether mathematics is true, bracketing it as a philosophical matter? Not so: the truth of mathematics is essential to science. It is hardly credible that scientists would devolve to philosophers the task of answering what according to the naturalist is a scientific question (surely scientists are adept at recognizing scientific questions) using scientific standards (surely scientists are adept at applying these standards), and one of great moment for the whole scientific

---

[50] Z is the ring of integers, Q the field of rationals, and A the field of algebraic numbers.

enterprise (surely scientists would feel honor-bound to tackle it themselves). The fact is that an equation such as

$$1 + c + c^2 + \ldots + c^n = \left(1 - c^{n+1}\right)/(1-c),$$

is accepted unreservedly by scientists acting as scientists (when $c \neq 1$, naturally). Similarly, as Putnam (2012, pp. 188–9) points out, no serious quantum field theorist doubts that the evolution of electrons and similar particles is by and large governed by the Dirac equation or some more precise equation which the Dirac equation approximates.

It is otherwise with the metaphysics of mathematics, for example with the claim that the number denoted by "c" in the preceding sum is abstract. Although scientists believe that mathematics is literally true, there is no reason to suppose they endorse its specifically platonist construal. It is no part of science as habitually practiced, for example, that "2 + 3 = 5" should be interpreted as being about some specific abstract objects (viz. 2, 3 and 5) and some specific abstract function or relation (viz. addition). The kinds of structuralist interpretations on the philosophical market would be seen by most scientists as scientifically on a par with literal construals.[51] These different conceptions of mathematical truth do not impinge on the practice of science. Underlying this sort of attitude is a view commonly held by scientists, and virtually everyone else for that matter. Mathematics, scientists believe, is an auxiliary to scientific endeavor rather than its subject matter. So although mathematics is indisputably true (scientists believe), what exactly its truth consists in is not an obviously scientific matter.

Now, the fact that the question of what mathematics is about is not addressed by, or even of relevance to, working scientists – beyond the fact that mathematical claims are true – does not mean that the question is not ultimately a scientific one. It could simply mean that the types of arguments needed to tackle it are much more general. They may be still scientific in a broad sense, though not of the type that scientists consciously deploy in everyday research.[52]

Our conclusion is that scientists typically do not test mathematical assumptions precisely because they blithely assume their truth. Very few scientists adopt an instrumentalist attitude to mathematics. Almost all of them assume the truth of mathematics and its reliability in scientific applications. When an

---

[51] We encountered one of these, eliminative structuralism, in Footnote 17: it construes a mathematical statement such as "2 + 3 = 5" as a claim about what holds in any structure that satisfies the axioms of arithmetic. For an introduction to structuralism in the philosophy of mathematics and its varieties, see Hellman and Shapiro (2019).

[52] For more extensive discussion of the gap between scientific confirmation of mathematical truth and scientific confirmation of platonism, see Paseau (2007).

astronomer uses mathematics to correctly calculate the next solar eclipse, they do not say to themselves, *sotto voce*, "God knows whether the mathematics I have relied on is true – but thankfully it gives me the right answer." They take the mathematical-physical package as true, which explains their confidence in their astronomical predictions. Naturally, some parts of successful scientific practice are more settled than others. But much mainstream mathematics is used in theories not only indispensable to best science but, moreover, unhesitatingly, unconditionally, and literally accepted by scientists. The scientific practice objection to the Indispensability Argument's first premise, in its different variants, looks quite resistible.

There is, however, another way to understand the scientific practice objection. We have construed it as a claim about what, literally, the practice of science involves. And as we saw, this practice involves commitment to mathematics, broadly speaking. The alternative construal is to read it as a claim about what scientific practice *should* involve. The question is not whether scientists *in fact* take mathematics literally (our answer: they do), but whether they *should* take it literally, given the role it plays in science. Would it not play the role equally well if it were, say, merely a useful fiction? This sort of question has prompted philosophers to focus their attention on the fine-grained role mathematics plays in scientific applications. As a result, the more recent debate has turned on an "enhanced" version of the Indispensability Argument.

5 The Enhanced Indispensability Argument

5.1 Moving Beyond the Quine–Putnam Indispensability Argument

The core of the scientific practice objection, as summarized in the previous section, is that two of the underpinnings of the Indispensability Argument, (confirmational) holism and naturalism, come into conflict with one another. On the one hand, holism dictates that we treat all of the indispensable posits of a theory as being on an ontological par. On the other hand, naturalism dictates that we differentiate between different indispensable posits based on their theoretical role. Maddy first raised this objection in the early 1990s. Fast forward another ten years to the early 2000s and we see echoes of Maddy's worry about holism and the Indispensability Argument in the "weaseling" arguments of Joseph Melia. Melia (2000) concedes that mathematics is indispensable for science, but not in the sort of role that carries ontological commitment. In particular, mathematics plays a descriptive role that "indexes" the physical properties which do the substantive theoretical work. In such contexts, Melia sees nothing irrational about "weaseling out" from commitment to the mathematical components of such descriptions. To give a simple example,

Melia sees nothing wrong in asserting, "The number of moons of Mars is two, and there are no numbers." For Melia, this is no more objectionable than asserting, for example, "This natural rock formation looks just like a dragon's head, and there are no dragons."

A feature that Maddy's scientific practice objection and Melia's weaseling approach have in common is that they do not depend on attacking the thesis that mathematics is indispensable for science. The Indispensability Argument's second premise is left alone, and instead the focus is on challenging the first premise and its linking of indispensability with ontological commitment. This is not to say that Maddy and Melia are in the same camp, philosophically speaking. Maddy is an arch-naturalist, and ends up defending her own distinctive view of mathematics which she calls *mathematical naturalism* (Maddy 1997). This is the view which, broadened and extended, turned into Maddy's Second Philosophy, outlined in Section 2.2. By contrast, Melia is a nominalist sympathizer, and is interested in making room for more straightforwardly anti-platonist views of mathematics. However, in terms of strategies for attacking the Indispensability Argument, the contrast between Maddy and Melia on the one hand, and Field on the other, is clear. Field's single-minded focus is on the Indispensability Argument's second premise, while he basically accepts the ontological consequences of indispensability as summarized in its first premise. The label "Hard Road Nominalism" is aptly applied to Field's strategy, since attacking the thesis that mathematics is indispensable for science is definitely hard! Indeed, as we saw in Section 3, it requires technical nominalistic reconstructions of large swathes of scientific theorizing.

From the perspective just outlined, Maddy's scientific practice objection can be seen as a precursor to an alternative style of argument against the Indispensability Argument that has come to be known as *Easy Road Nominalism*. Melia's weaseling approach is a canonical example of Easy Road Nominalism, and henceforth we will apply this label more generally to any line of argument against the Indispensability Argument that leaves its second premise alone and focuses instead on undermining the first. Influential though Field's approach has been, few other nominalists have followed him down the Hard Road Nominalist path. Increasingly, it has been the Easy Road that has drawn opponents of the Indispensability Argument and its platonist consequences.

What implications does this have for platonist defenders of the Indispensability Argument? In many respects, the argument's first premise seems to be more vulnerable to attack than the second. To be sure, part of the appeal of Easy Road Nominalism as a strategy for nominalistic attack on the argument is that engagement with the logical complexities of nominalistic reconstruction can for the most part be avoided. But there are also other reasons that are less purely pragmatic.

Firstly, when it comes to the cogency of the second premise, the burden of proof can reasonably be presumed to be on the nominalist. For it is unquestionably the case that large amounts of mathematical apparatus are used in science; moreover, in nearly all cases it is far from straightforward to see how the mathematics could be removed without fatally weakening the scientific theory in which it features. Secondly, the nominalist is making what is effectively a universally generalized counterclaim: that for every current (and future) scientific theory, it is possible to formulate a fully adequate version of the theory that does not quantify over mathematical objects. A universal claim of this sort is by nature fragile, since a single counterexample is sufficient to overturn it. Thus, for example, it would not be enough for the Hard Road critic of the Indispensability Argument to provide successful nominalistic reconstructions of 99 out of 100 scientific theories if the 100th theory could not also be nominalized.[53]

When it comes to the plausibility of the first premise, by contrast, the burden-of-proof situation is more or less reversed. Here the platonist proponent of the Indispensability Argument is tasked with defending a thesis which, as currently formulated, maintains a normative connection between indispensability for science and ontological commitment that holds universally. This puts the platonist on the defensive, since a single type of context in which this link is plausibly broken would be enough to cast doubt on the entire Indispensability Argument.

Viewing the dialectical situation through this lens makes it unsurprising that nominalists have increasingly sought to shift the terrain of battle over the Indispensability Argument from its second to its first premise. At the same time, this perspective can also be used by the platonist to provide strategic insights on how best to respond to nominalists who follow the Easy Road. If the first premise's vulnerability stems mainly from the generality – perhaps over-generality – of its central claim, then a natural move is to look and see if the scope of the claim can be narrowed.

---

[53] It is worth noting that not everything about the premise is stacked in favor of the platonist. In particular, a claim of indispensability is effectively a *modal* claim, and a strong one at that. It is difficult to see how any individual claim – say that mathematical apparatus m^* is indispensable in scientific theory s^* – could ever be established conclusively, since it is always conceivable that a nominalizing scheme could be devised at some point in the future. (Bangu [2012, p. 77] makes a very similar point.)

As we have seen, Quine himself endorses a blanket holism that leaves him relatively unconcerned about the precise ways in which individual posits are indispensable. For Quine, the way to discover our commitments is to regiment our best scientific theories. Surveying the results, we ought to be committed to the objects over which the (first-order) quantifiers range. Putnam seconds Quine (minus the insistence on first-order regimentation): "It is silly to agree that a reason for believing that p warrants accepting p in all scientific circumstances, and then to add 'but even so it is not good enough'" (Putnam 1971, p. 356).

The Quine–Putnam approach, also shared by Field, leaves no room for instrumentalism of the type gestured at by the Easy Road nominalist. To borrow a famous saying of Russell's, instrumentalism has the advantages of theft over honest toil. However, it is far from clear that the full Quinean backdrop is necessary in order for an effective indispensability-based argument for mathematical platonism to go through. Recall that the principal target of Maddy's scientific practice objection in Section 4 was Quine's blanket appeal to (confirmational) holism. It is this holism that underpins the very general linking of indispensability to ontological commitment in the original argument's first premise.

Combining these considerations opens the way to the following strategic modification to the Indispensability Argument, whose original version – and the one discussed up to this point in the Element – we shall now refer to as the "Quine–Putnam Indispensability Argument" or QPIA. The idea is to make the normative claim of the first premise more defensible by narrowing the kind of theoretical role whose indispensability carries ontological commitment. In other words, rather than claiming very generally that indispensability entails ontological commitment, the claim is made that indispensability *for theoretical role*, R^*, entails ontological commitment. If we can find a role, R^*, for which this claim is plausible, and furthermore show that some mathematical posits are indispensable for R^*, then we have the makings of an indispensability-based argument for platonism that will be significantly more resilient against nominalist attack. It is interesting that Melia, the preeminent nominalist opponent of QPIA, explicitly endorses the in-principle effectiveness of this line of argument: "Were there clear examples where the postulation of mathematics objects results in an increase in the same kind of utility as that provided by the postulation of theoretical entities, then it would seem that the same kind of considerations that support the existence of atoms, electrons and space-time equally supports [sic] the existence of numbers, functions and sets" (Melia 2002, pp. 75–6).

5.2 The Enhanced Indispensability Argument

So much for schematics. What should this narrowed role, R^*, actually be? One candidate for R^* stands out, given the implicit endorsement of scientific realism by both sides in the debate over QPIA, and this is *explanation*. A lynchpin of scientific realism is inference to the best explanation, which is appealed to in order to justify the postulation of unobservable concrete posits such as electrons and black holes. If we reformulate inference to the best explanation in terms of indispensability, then this amounts to saying that the scientific realist believes in the existence of electrons because electrons play an indispensable explanatory role in science.[54]

The centrality of explanatory considerations for the scientific realist is hardly surprising, nor is the fact that indispensabilist platonists piggyback on appeals to inference to the best explanation in order to justify the existence of abstract mathematical objects. What is striking, however, is that the key nominalist opponents of QPIA also endorse inference to the best explanation. This is true of both the Hard Road nominalist, Field, and the Easy Road nominalist, Melia. Thus Field writes that the key issue in the platonism-nominalism debate is "one special kind of indispensability argument: one involving indispensability *for explanations*" (Field 1989, p. 14; italics in the original). Melia is also fairly explicit that what matters is explanation (Melia 2000), and he mentions explanatory power as an important theoretical virtue (Melia 2002, p. 75). Melia is doubtful, however, whether mathematics ever plays a genuinely explanatory role in science.

The new revised version of QPIA, focusing on explanatory role, has come to be known as the *Enhanced Indispensability Argument*, and is standardly formulated as follows:[55]

The Enhanced Indispensability Argument (EIA)

1. We ought rationally to believe in the existence of any entity which plays an indispensable explanatory role in our best scientific theories.
2. Mathematical objects play an indispensable explanatory role in science.

We ought rationally to believe in the existence of mathematical objects.

---

[54] Of course, some scientific realists will go further and argue that what is crucial here is that electrons play an indispensable explanatory role in *causal* explanations. We will return to the putative role of causality in Section 6.3.

[55] This label was introduced in Baker (2005). The argument is also sometimes referred to as the "Explanatory Indispensability Argument" (thus, conveniently, also abbreviated to EIA), especially by those who harbor doubts about whether it really is an enhancement of the original Quine–Putnam version of the argument.

5.3 The Role of Case Studies in Supporting EIA

Unlike the broad indispensability claim, the claim that mathematics specifically plays an indispensable *explanatory* role in science is neither obvious nor uncontentious. Hence it needs to be defended. And defending the claim is not something that can be done purely in principle. Actual examples of (clearly) indispensable, explanatory mathematics need to be exhibited.

The shift of attention from QPIA to EIA over the past two decades has therefore been accompanied by an increasing focus on case studies of putative explanatory uses of mathematics in science. This has been a welcome move for several reasons, not least of which is a much closer engagement with actual scientific and mathematical practice than was true in the heyday of QPIA. Detailed examination of case studies also has the potential to uncover varieties of subroles that mathematical apparatus may play within the broader category of explanatory role.

Here we will restrict our attention to just one of these numerous case studies, involving the life cycles of periodical cicadas. This was introduced into the philosophical literature in Baker (2005) and is probably the most discussed case study in the debate over EIA.[56] Three species of North American cicada of the genus *Magicicada*, known as "periodical cicadas," share the same unusual life cycle. In each species the nymphal stage remains in the soil for a lengthy period, then the adult cicada emerges after either 13 years or 17 years depending on the geographical area. Even more strikingly, this emergence is synchronized among all members of a cicada species in any given area. The adults all emerge within the same few days, they mate, die a few weeks later and then the cycle repeats itself. One key question to be answered is the following: why are the life-cycle periods *prime*? In other words, given a synchronized, periodic life-cycle, is there some evolutionary advantage to having a period that is prime? If so, this would help explain why 13 and 17 are the favored cycle periods for each of the three species of the genus *Magicicada*. In seeking to answer this question, biologists have come up with two basic alternative theories.

An explanation of the advantage of prime cycle periods has been offered by Goles, Schulz, and Markus (2001) based on avoiding predators.[57] Goles et al. hypothesize an epoch in the evolutionary past of *Magicicada* when it was attacked by predators that were themselves periodic, with lower cycle periods. Clearly it is advantageous – other things being equal – for the cicada species to intersect as rarely as possible with such predators. The authors' claim is that the

---

[56] This summary of the cicada case study is taken from the presentation given in Baker (2005).

[57] This was the first mathematical model to appear in the literature, but the argument linking prime periods to predator avoidance is older, and goes at least as far back as Gould (1977).

frequency of intersection is minimized when the cicada's period is prime: "For example, a prey with a 12-year cycle will meet – every time it appears – properly synchronized predators appearing every 1, 2, 3, 4, 6 or 12 years, whereas a mutant with a 13-year period has the advantage of being subject to fewer predators" (Goles, Schulz, and Markus 2001, p. 33).

The mathematical underpinnings of both the predation and the hybridization explanations lie in number theory, the branch of mathematics which investigates the often deep and subtle relationships between the integers. The mathematical link between primality and minimizing the intersection of periods involves the notion of *lowest common multiple* (lcm). The lcm of two natural numbers, m and n, is the smallest number into which both m and n divide exactly; for example, the lcm of 4 and 10 is 20. Assume that m and n are the life-cycle periods (in years) of two subspecies of cicada, C_m and C_n. If C_m and C_n intersect in a particular year, then the year of their next intersection is given by the lcm of m and n. In other words, the lcm is the number of years between successive intersections.

In fact, the fundamental property in this context is not primality but *coprimality*; two numbers, m and n, are coprime if they have no common factors other than 1. All that is needed to underpin the predation and hybridization explanations are the following two number-theoretic results:

Lemma 1: the lowest common multiple of m and n is less than or equal to $m.n$, and it is equal to this upper bound if and only if m and n are coprime.[58]

Lemma 1 implies that the intersection frequency of two periods of length m and n is maximized when m and n are coprime. We get from coprimality to primality *simpliciter* with a second result:

Lemma 2: a number, m, is coprime with each number $n < 2m, n \neq m$ if and only if m is prime.

The mathematics for the predation explanation is already contained in these two Lemmas. Predators are assumed to have relatively short cycle periods. It therefore suffices to show that prime numbers maximize their lcm relative to all lower numbers. More formally, we need to show that for a given prime, p, and for any pair of numbers, m and n, both less than p, the lcm of p and m is greater than the lcm of n and m. But this follows directly from Lemmas 1 and 2. Furthermore, only prime numbers maximize their lcms in this way, so in this respect primes are optimal.

---

[58] For proofs of all lemmas, see Landau (1958).

Plugging the cicada explanation into Premise 2 of the Enhanced Indispensability Argument yields the following "cicada-specific" version of the Indispensability Thesis:

(2)$_{CIC}$ Mathematical objects play an indispensable explanatory role in the best scientific explanation of cicada period lengths.

5.4 The Audience for EIA

As we have seen, QPIA has been challenged on two main fronts. A follower of the Hard Road (for example, Hartry Field) aims to show that mathematical entities such as numbers are not in fact indispensable. A follower of the Easy Road (for example, Joseph Melia) aims to show that the theoretical roles of electrons and numbers are importantly different.

EIA also draws on an analogy between numbers and electrons, but it does so based on a much more specific similarity between the respective theoretical roles of these two kinds of entity. It is not merely that numbers and electrons both appear as indispensable posits in our best overall theory, it is that both play an *explanatory* role within the theory. Thus a sweeping appeal to holism no longer needs to be made.[59] Instead, appeal is made to inference to the best explanation. The challenge that EIA poses to anti-platonists can then be put in the form of a question: on what principled grounds ought inference to the best explanation to the existence of mathematical objects be blocked?

The intended target of EIA is any philosopher who is both a scientific realist and a nominalist. Consider one such person, call her Ronni.[60] As a scientific realist, Ronni believes in the existence of well-established concrete theoretical posits in science such as electrons, quarks, and black holes. As a nominalist, Ronni does not believe in the existence of any abstract objects, including abstract mathematical objects such as numbers, functions, and sets. EIA aims to put pressure on Ronni by arguing that she has the *same* kind of grounds for believing in numbers that she has for believing in electrons. In both cases, the entities in question play an indispensable role in explaining certain observable phenomena. Hence inference to the best explanation should be applied in both cases to deduce the existence of the corresponding entities. Viewed from this perspective, EIA is a kind of "leveraging" argument. It aims to convert scientific realists into mathematical platonists by leveraging their belief in the existence of electrons into belief about the existence of numbers.

---

[59] The "sweeping" qualifier here is important, for there are some philosophers who believe that EIA still requires some kind of holism in order to be successful against the nominalist. See, for example, Bangu (2012, chapter 3).

[60] For **R**ealist plus **N**ominalist.

Recall that the purpose of the move from the Quine–Putnam Indispensability Argument to the Enhanced Indispensability Argument is to sharpen the first premise of the argument and thus make it easier to fend off nominalist attacks. The success of this strategy with respect to Hard Road Nominalism and Easy Road Nominalism will be assessed in the next two sections. However, not all attacks on QPIA are blunted by this move. To give the most obvious example, since EIA involves using scientific realism to put pressure on nominalism, a nominalist who is *not* a scientific realist is likely to be unmoved. This point holds equally for both QPIA and EIA. Consider, for example, a constructive empiricist nominalist, call him Connor.[61] Following the van Fraassen line, Connor our constructive empiricist does not take on ontological commitment to unobservables and so does not believe in the existence of electrons. Thus Connor can accept the indispensabilist conditional that if we ought to believe in electrons then we ought to believe in numbers, while at the same time rejecting both its antecedent and its consequent!

No philosophical argument is effective for all audiences, and the Enhanced Indispensability Argument is no exception. The importance of EIA stems from the fact that scientific realism (in some form) is a popular philosophical position, and in particular that alternatives to scientific realism that reject ontological commitment to unobservables are very much in the minority. In the domain of mathematics, by contrast, philosophers seem more evenly divided over whether to endorse platonism or to support one of the anti-realist alternatives that fall under the umbrella of nominalism.[62]

6 Easy Road Fictionalism

6.1 Narrowing the Easy Road

An "Easy Road" position against a given version of an indispensability-based argument takes exception to its first premise. Easy Road Nominalism, as deployed against QPIA, is based on the claim that mere indispensability is not sufficient for ontological commitment. Rather what is required is playing an indispensable *explanatory role*. The Enhanced Indispensability Argument blocks this route, because Premise 1 of EIA is acceptable to proponents of Easy Road Nominalism.

Is there still an "Easy Road" available to (scientific realist) critics of EIA? Perhaps, but this road is now considerably narrower. As scientific realists,

---

[61] For Constructive Empiricist plus Nominalist.

[62] There are also other alternatives to platonism that are not clearly anti-realist, such as logicism, structuralism, and mathematical naturalism.

proponents of the Easy Road must accept inference to the best explanation as a prima facie reliable mode of inference. However, "prima facie reliable" is different from "universally applicable," so there may still be some room for maneuver. In the remainder of this section, we survey three kinds of strategy that have been adopted in pursuit of the Easy Road against EIA. The first strategy is to present examples of clearly nonexistent entities that play an indispensable explanatory role in science, which would show that inference to the best explanation does not always hold. The second strategy is to argue that there are principled restrictions on the scope of such inferences, or on the type of explanatory role that supports them. And the third strategy is to accept that inference to the best explanation is always a rational mode of inference, but that it can be overridden by other considerations.

In order to avoid confusion with Easy Road arguments against QPIA, we shall henceforth refer to the Easy Road position against EIA as "Easy Road Fictionalism." As well as marking the difference between these two kinds of position (in particular, that Easy Road Nominalism accepts inference to the best explanation unrestrictedly, while Easy Road Fictionalism does not), it also fits with the evolution in how anti-platonists describe their own positions. It is more common to find recent defenders of Easy Road approaches against EIA describing themselves as fictionalists rather than nominalists, partly because they may not be committed to a full-fledged nominalism that extends beyond the rejection of abstract mathematical objects.

6.2 Nonexistent Entities Are Sometimes Explanatory

Part of the motivation for Easy Road Nominalism involved citing examples of (clearly) nonexistent entities that play an indispensable role in science. It will be helpful (though perhaps not absolutely essential) to the Easy Road fictionalist case to – analogously – find examples of nonexistent entities that play an indispensable *explanatory* role. In this section, we will focus on what is probably the most frequently cited putative example of such entities, namely, idealized concrete posits such as infinitely thin strings and perfectly continuous fluids.

A prominent proponent of Easy Road Fictionalism is Mary Leng.[63] In Section 4.2, we discussed one of her key arguments, which makes explicit reference to idealizations. We saw there that it is not plausible to think that scientists take mathematics to be an idealization. We now reprise this argument

---

[63] The following discussion of Leng's position derives from Baker (2012).

in light of our renewed focus on explanation. Schematically, Leng's positive argument for Easy Road Fictionalism runs as follows:

1. Idealizations and mathematical entities both play an indispensable role in scientific explanations.
2. But even scientific realists do not believe in the existence of idealizations, hence there is more to ontological commitment than just explanatory role.

Notice that this argument can be run even if, as we saw Section 4.2, scientists do not liken mathematics to a scientific idealization.

Leng starts with the plausible thesis that even scientific realists ought to want to avoid ontological commitment to idealizations such as point masses and frictionless surfaces (Leng 2010, p. 42). She discusses elimination strategies for such idealizations, in particular the Quinean strategy of parsing claims involving idealizations as shorthand claims for what happens as a certain limit is approached (Leng 2010, p. 117). Following Maddy, Leng argues that this will not work for all idealizations. For example, the assumption – commonly made in fluid dynamics – that fluids are continuous does not predict the behavior of actual fluids as they get closer and closer to being genuinely continuous (Leng 2010, p. 118).

Assume that Leng is correct about the indispensability of the assumption that fluids are continuous. The key question – for defending Easy Road Fictionalism – is whether idealizing assumptions of this sort play an indispensable *explanatory* role in science. Here is what Leng says about this issue: "[G]iven that our current best explanation of the dynamic behaviour of fluids is that they act *as if* they were continuous, it is arguable that any alternative literally believed theory of fluids, which dropped the comparison with continuous ideal fluids, would suffer a loss in explanatory power" (Leng 2010, p. 120).

The reason that Leng gives for why the comparison with continuous ideal fluids is explanatory is that it ignores the detailed molecular structure of individual fluids. It therefore has more generality than a more fine-grained "literally believed theory of fluids."

Worries may legitimately be raised here about the extent to which the comparison with continuous ideal fluids is doing real explanatory work. Perhaps the easiest way to articulate this worry is by focusing on the why-question (or questions) these idealizations are being invoked to answer. Leng's sample why-question is the following: why do all fluids (of the relevant sort) behave similarly despite their differing molecular structures? Her putative answer is that "these fluids behave similarly because they all behave *as if* they are continuous" (Leng 2010, p. 120). Taken on its own, this surely fails to be a genuine explanation. There are at least two problems. Firstly, it seems to merely redescribe the way in which the various fluids are similar, as opposed to explaining their common behavior.[64] Secondly, no actual property of any of the fluids is cited. Consider the following amended explanation: these fluids behave similarly because the size of their constituent elements is very small relative to their volume, hence they behave as if they are continuous. This looks to be closer to a genuine explanation, and it includes a reference to (presumably ideal) continuous fluids. Is this enough to make Leng's point?

Focusing on this reformulated explanation raises a new worry, however, namely whether the reference to continuous fluids is doing any real explanatory work. What is lost if we just shorten the explanation? In other words, if we say that the fluids behave similarly because the size of their constituent elements is very small relative to their volume. To be sure, a mathematical model involving perfectly continuous fluids will be helpful in predicting the behavior of various actual fluids. But is it not facts about the actual properties of these fluids, such as the small size of their constituents, that is doing the real explanatory work?[65]

Another version of Easy Road Fictionalism that has important similarities to Leng's is the "mathematical figuralism" of Stephen Yablo (1998, 2000, 2005, 2012). On Yablo's view, scientific language contains figurative, as well as literal, parts. Since there is no hope of separating the first from the second, there is no hope of isolating the parts of science that carry ontological commitment from those that do not. In response, one might concede that it is not always possible to sift the literal from the metaphorical in a scientific claim or explanation. But we usually have a good sense of what literal account a scientific metaphor is standing as a proxy for. Metaphors in mathematics are easily and customarily eliminated.[66] The same goes for science. No physicist worth their salt will rest content with a metaphorical explanation whose literal content eludes them, even if a clean separation of metaphor from literal description would be tricky. Honest fictionalists must therefore provide literal proxies for metaphorical explanations they regard as essential to best science. Otherwise it is doubtful that these explanations should count as part of best science. This line of counterargument against Easy Road Fictionalism is due to

---

[64] One source of confusion is that we do sometimes use the term "explain" in cases where we are really describing. For example, I may explain where Naples is by referring to Italy as a boot.

[65] It is worth noting that this line of response is a potentially risky one for the platonist, since a nominalist could turn this argument around and assert that, in the case of putative mathematical explanations in science, it is really the physical facts that are doing the explanatory work.

[66] See the discussion of metaphor in Paseau (forthcoming, b).

Mark Colyvan, who concludes his critique of Yablo with the following declaration: "[W]hen some piece of language is delivering an explanation, either that piece of language must be interpreted literally or the non-literal reading of the language in question stands proxy for the real explanation" (Colyvan 2010, p. 16).

Colyvan's challenge has real force, and in the current context it raises the following dilemma for an Easy Road position such as Leng's. Either a candidate explanation makes reference to a bare idealization – in other words a face-value reference to something that does not exist – in which case it is false and thus not a genuine explanation, or a candidate explanation links the idealization to some actual property, in which case the idealization is dispensable from the explanation.

The upshot of this discussion is that Leng has yet to make a good case for any idealized entities playing an explanatory role in science. However, even if she were successful, would this be enough to sever the link between explanation and ontological commitment? Not necessarily. As Leng herself points out, there are two ways of understanding the claim that some idealized entity, for example a perfectly continuous fluid, exists. One way to take this claim is as saying that some actual, physical fluids are perfectly continuous. On this interpretation, even the realist will presumably agree that the claim is false. However, another way to understand the claim is as being about the existence of an *abstract* entity. A continuous fluid is conceived of as part of a mathematical model of a certain kind, a model which – by assumption – plays an essential role in some scientific explanation (Leng 2010, p. 113). In this situation, however, it seems perfectly plausible for the mathematical realist to accept the truth of the claim that continuous fluids exist. For the fluid in question is essentially a mathematical entity, and this is precisely the way – according to the proponent of EIA – that ontological commitment to such entities arises.

Leng seems to accept that such a position is coherent, but she argues that her fictionalist position is more plausible. Her main argument focuses on *dispensable* idealizations, such as frictionless planes. She writes that "we seemingly manage to achieve something by speaking as if there are ideal, frictionless planes even though, according to our *best* physical theory, we need not assume that there are such things" (Leng 2010, p. 136). Hence, Leng suggests, we ought to expect that there is some account of "the success of our theory of frictionless planes" that does not assume that such abstract entities exist (Leng 2010, p. 126). Once again, however, Leng slides here from the issue of explanatory role in particular to more general talk of "theoretical success." One might argue, contra Leng, that our demonstration of the dispensability of frictionless slopes goes hand in hand with our recognition that such entities do not play a genuine explanatory role in science.

6.3 Restricting Inference to the Best Explanation

Let us now move to a second potential strategy for the Easy Road fictionalist, which is to argue that there are principled restrictions on the scope of inference to the best explanation.

One version of this strategy begins by distinguishing between different notions of explanation and then arguing that only a subset of these notions supports the derivation of ontological commitment. The most common such distinction is between ontic explanation and epistemic explanation. On this view, *M epistemically explains P* if we can understand *P* by thinking in terms of *M*, and *M ontically explains P* only if *M* is related to *P* via some real physical relation.[67] The fact that an entity plays an indispensable epistemic explanatory role in science is not in itself enough to justify ontological commitment. This opens the way for the Easy Road fictionalist to argue that mathematical apparatus only ever plays an epistemic explanatory role in science, and hence ontological commitment to mathematical objects can be justifiably avoided.[68]

The supporter of EIA has several avenues available for resisting this second strategy. For a start, proponents of a distinction between epistemic and ontic explanation need to do some work to establish that there is a genuine distinction to be made here, and they also need to demonstrate that mathematical explanations always fall on the epistemic side of the divide. There is also the issue of fitting with scientific practice. The burden of proof here is on the fictionalist side to show that scientists do in fact – whether explicitly or implicitly – make a substantive distinction between ontologically committing and non–ontologically committing modes of explanation.

A cruder version of this second strategy can be found in what are sometimes referred to as "Eleatic Arguments," which are arguments to the effect that inference to the best explanation only applies to *causal* entities.[69] Problems similar to those mentioned here arise with showing that such a restriction tracks actual scientific practice. If anything, the situation is

---

[67] For versions of this distinction, in the context of arguing against indispensability-based arguments for platonism, see, for example, Marcus (2014), Molinini (2016), Vineberg (2018), and Knowles and Saatsi (2019). For more on the ontic conception in particular, see Craver (2014).

[68] Another related "divide and conquer" approach is due to Stephen Yablo. Yablo argues that there are three levels of explanatory involvement that an entity can have. The fact that an entity has indispensable explanatory involvement at level 1 or level 2 is not enough to justify ontological commitment. See Yablo (2012).

[69] For a useful survey of these arguments, see Colyvan (2001, chapter 3).

worse. Scientists certainly use inference to the best explanation to infer the existence of entities that are not causally active *with us*; for example, stars and galaxies outside our light cone. So if causal interaction with us is not a necessary condition for the legitimate postulation of entities, it is unclear why lack of causal activity *tout court* should be a disqualifying condition, as per the Eleatic argument.[70]

A variation on the second strategy for the Easy Road fictionalist, which may or may not qualify as a third separate strategy, is to accept that inference to the best explanation is always a rational mode of inference, but to argue that inference to the best explanation can sometimes be overridden by other considerations. As one example, some philosophers have claimed that we ought to draw ontological conclusions from our best explanations of scientific phenomena unless the existence of the entities in question makes no difference to the concrete, physical world.[71] This is sometimes referred to as the *Makes No Difference* (MND) argument, and, when deployed against indispensabilist arguments for platonism, MND can be formulated as follows:

1. If there were no mathematical objects then (according to platonism) this would make no difference to the concrete, physical world.
2. Hence (on the platonist picture) we have no reason to believe in the existence of mathematical objects.

Henceforth, we shall refer to the premise of the MND argument as "(No-Difference)." At first blush, (No-Difference) seems hard to resist. Surely it is obvious that mathematical objects – if acausal and nonspatiotemporal – make no difference to the arrangement of the concrete world?[72]

Jody Azzouni and Mark Balaguer have – separately – offered two formulations of the same quick argument for (No-Difference), based on the acausal nature of mathematical objects. This argument is put in terms of what would (or would not) happen if mathematical objects suddenly ceased to exist. Azzouni, for example, asks us to "[i]magine that mathematical

---

[70] Another variation on this second approach, which places a slightly different restriction on inference to the best explanation, is to maintain that we ought to draw ontological conclusions from our best explanations of scientific phenomena only if the entities in question play an epistemic role in our theories (see Azzouni 1994)

[71] This presentation of the MND argument originally appeared in Baker (2003).

[72] It is worth noting that the issues of difference-making and explanation intersect with one another, and that aspects of this intersection are explored, for example, in Woodward (2003) and in Strevens (2011). For example, it may be that the claim "x makes no difference to y" implies "x does not explain y," in which case any genuine case of mathematical explanation in science would imply a corresponding difference-making claim.

objects ceased to exist sometime in 1968. Mathematical work went on as usual. Why wouldn't it?" (Azzouni 1994, p. 56)[73] Meanwhile, Balaguer writes that "if all the objects in the mathematical realm suddenly disappeared, nothing would change in the physical world" (Balaguer 1998, p. 132).

This is less an argument than an appeal to raw intuitions. It is not relied heavily upon by either author; however, it is important because the underlying intuition is both widely held and potentially misleading. The intuition to which Azzouni and Balaguer appeal is the following: since mathematical objects are by hypothesis acausal, if they were suddenly to blink out of existence then this would have no "knock-on" effects on the concrete, physical world. A moment's reflection, however, shows that this line of reasoning has no real force. Central to the platonist account is that mathematical objects are nonspatiotemporal, and it is incoherent to hypothesize that an atemporal object suddenly ceases to exist in 1968. The "blinking-out" argument focuses on the acausality of abstract mathematical objects, but in doing so it implicitly attributes temporal properties to them.[74]

This sort of looseness is symptomatic of a general tendency to view abstract objects as akin to ultra-remote, ultra-inert concrete objects. For there is nothing incoherent about imagining concrete objects blinking out of existence. Nor is it only temporal properties that get inadvertently attributed to mathematical abstracta. A similar phenomenon occurs with spatial properties. It is all too easy, for example, to slip from talking of mathematical objects as being nonspatiotemporal to talking of them as existing outside of space-time. But "outside" is of course a spatial notion, hence it cannot legitimately be applied to abstract mathematical objects. Talking this way encourages the picture of mathematical abstracta existing in some distant realm, a realm which is further from us than even the remotest concrete object.[75] An analogous slide occurs with respect to the acausal nature of abstract objects. This feature is often glossed by saying that abstract objects are not causally active, or – more equivocally – that they are "causally inert." However, causal inertness, like

---

[73] It should be noted that in more recent work, Azzouni has explicitly distanced himself from a strict ontological interpretation of this "blinking-out" thought experiment (Azzouni 2000).

[74] One could imagine versions of platonism according to which mathematical objects have temporal properties, and thus can in principle blink out of (and into) existence. Such versions might be open to the Balaguer–Azzouni argument. Nonetheless, the standard platonist position is certainly that mathematical objects are neither spatial nor temporal, and this is a consensus with which both Azzouni and Balaguer explicitly agree.

[75] "If I assert details of the inhabitants of a distant planet but deny that I have any knowledge of those aliens, then there is no reason why my assertions should be regarded as anything more than idle fancies" (Cheyne 1998, p. 34).

remoteness, is a property which can be possessed (to varying degrees) by concrete objects. For example, some gases are classed as inert because they do not easily react with other substances. This again encourages a view of abstract objects that places them at the end of a continuum of cases incorporating successively more inert concrete objects.

The blinking-out argument, even if it were coherent, provides no quick route to establishing the "no" position. The principal reason is that it appeals to intuitions which are derived from, and thus uncontroversially only have force for, concrete objects. One moral to be drawn from this is that the (No-Difference) claim must be understood as a timeless counterfactual. The issue, in other words, is not whether the existence, here and now, of mathematical objects makes a difference, but whether their existence, in the unrestricted and timeless sense appropriate to mathematical objects, makes a difference.

The third route to Easy Road Fictionalism depends, therefore, on the truth of the timeless counterfactual claim that if there were no mathematical objects then the concrete, physical world would be just as it is. And the problem for Easy Road Fictionalism is that this third route may have to detour onto the Hard Road in order to defend this key counterfactual. Why? Because the indispensabilist platonist can reasonably argue that if mathematics is indeed indispensable for science, then the counterfactual may well be false. A standard way of evaluating counterfactuals is using David Lewis' notion of similarity across possible worlds. We consider the most similar world to the actual world in which the antecedent of the counterfactual holds, and then check to see if the consequent is also true in that world.[76] However, it is also part of Lewis' framework that global differences between worlds matter more than local differences when it comes to assessing similarity. Consider a situation in which mathematics is indispensable for the formulation of one or more of the laws of nature in the actual world. Any possible world in which there are no mathematical objects would then be a world in which there are violations of the laws of nature of the actual world. How to determine the most similar such world to the actual world then becomes considerably more complicated.[77] Regardless of what the correct analysis turns out to be, it seems clear that the pursuer of this third route to Easy

---

[76] Note that this timeless counterfactual is in any case problematic from the traditional platonist point of view, because mathematical objects are taken to exist necessarily and thus the counterfactual at issue would feature a metaphysically impossible antecedent. On Lewis' semantics, all such "counterpossible" counterfactuals come out as trivially true. There are ways around this, for example by extending the Lewis semantics and adding impossible worlds. In any case, indispensabilist platonists tend to abandon the thesis that mathematical objects exist necessarily, so they can sidestep this particular issue. (Colyvan is one example of an indispensabilist platonist in this camp.)

[77] For further discussion of how to evaluate the timeless "No-Difference" counterfactual, see Baker (2003).

Road Fictionalism will need to engage substantially with the second premise of EIA and thus take some necessary steps along the Hard Road.[78]

It is important to the defense of the Enhanced Indispensability Argument, and against Easy Road Fictionalism, that idealized concrete posits and mathematical objects do not fall into the same category, explanation-wise. The Easy Road fictionalist maintains that both idealizations and mathematical objects play an indispensable explanatory role in science. This matching of theoretical role then provides motivation for restricting or overriding the force of inference to the best explanation, and thus resisting the platonist conclusion of EIA. The defender of EIA, by contrast, argues that mathematical objects play an indispensable explanatory role but that concrete idealizations do not. A third option is to deny that either concrete idealizations or abstract mathematical objects play an indispensable explanatory role in science. This is Hard Road Fictionalism, and it is to this stance that we turn in the next section.

7 Hard Road Fictionalism

7.1 Three Grades of Hard Road Fictionalism

For present purposes, Hard Road Fictionalism is defined as any approach to resisting the Enhanced Indispensability Argument that

- Accepts Premise 1 of EIA.
- Attacks Premise 2 of EIA on philosophical rather than scientific grounds.
- Aims to undermine Premise 2 by providing some alternative, mathematical-object-free apparatus that achieves the same specified goals.

As with earlier Field-style Hard Road Nominalism (against QPIA), Hard Road fictionalist attacks on EIA will typically involve some technical or logical work, in the form of reconstructions of key parts of our current scientific theories. It is this aspect which earns Hard Road Fictionalism its "Hard Road" label. In one important respect, however, Hard Road Fictionalism is a less daunting route for the anti-platonist than Hard Road Nominalism. The nominalist version of the Hard Road is tasked with showing the dispensability of mathematics from science *tout court*, while the fictionalist version need only show this for places where mathematics plays an explanatory role. The

---

[78] Another reason for thinking that this detour along the Hard Road is necessary relates to the point made earlier about the connection between difference-making and explanation. If explanation requires difference-making, then any claim of explanatory indispensability implies that (No-Difference) is false.

defender of EIA is banking on even this more tractable Hard Road being unfeasible to traverse.[79]

Since the focus of EIA is on explanatory role, the corresponding focus of Hard Road Fictionalism is on reconstructing mathematical explanations in a way that avoids quantifying over mathematical objects. A key question concerns what aspects of the original explanation need to be preserved in order for the reconstructed explanation to count as "scientifically adequate." In what follows, we will distinguish – and briefly discuss – three grades of Hard Road fictionalism, characterized according to what aspects of the content of the original explanation are taken by the fictionalist to require preservation.[80]

7.2 Nonmathematical Consequence-Preserving Hard Road Fictionalism

The first and most straightforward goal that the Hard Road fictionalist can set is to preserve the *nonmathematical* consequences of the original explanation. In other words, given a mathematical explanation, M, and a nominalistically reconstructed explanation, N, N is an adequate replacement for M only if every nonmathematical fact explained by M is also explained by N.

Several philosophers have argued against the cicada example from this kind of Hard Road fictionalist perspective, including Juha Saatsi, Chris Daly, and Simon Langford (Saatsi 2011; Daly and Langford 2009). Their aim is to reproduce nominalistically the local implications of whatever mathematical result is appealed to in the original explanation. In the case of the cicada explanation, the local implication is that, among (cicada) periods between 12 and 18, only 13 and 17 maximize their lcm with all (predator) periods less than 12. As these authors have noted, this can be verified by exhaustively checking through all the possible combinations of period lengths. Moreover, this can be done without bringing in any concept of primality, coprimality, or other essentially mathematical notions.

The basic idea behind the nonmathematical consequence-preserving Hard Road fictionalist strategy is to argue that we ought to be starting with an explanandum that is more specific. Thus, Juha Saatsi writes: "the point is that the explanandum of the biological theory is only that the periods are 13 or 17, not that the period is some n, where n is prime" (personal communication, by email, April 20, 2007). If this is right, so the thinking goes, then it may open the

---

[79] It is also unclear how much easier this revised Hard Road actually is in comparison to Hard Road Nominalism. In *Science Without Numbers*, Field emphasizes the importance of explanatory role, and it may well be that the places where mathematics plays an explanatory role in science are also among the hardest to nominalize.

[80] The following discussion draws on Baker (2016).

way to alternative, non-number-theoretic explanations. One possibility is a quasi-geometrical explanation, using physical objects as "props." Saatsi suggests using sets of sticks of different lengths, measured out in some given unit. We could lay a series of sticks of length 13 end to end, next to another series of sticks of some other length, say 14, and see how many sticks we have to lay down before the two series are the same length. We could repeat this for other integer unit lengths close to 13, and show that 13 and 17 require the longest series of sticks compared to other nearby lengths.

A second alternative that avoids invoking primality, suggested by Chris Daly and Simon Langford, is to seek an *intrinsic* explanation based on the precise details of each cicada subspecies' ecological past.

> "Why ... is the periodic life-cycle of *this* duration rather than any other?" This question focuses on the physical phenomenon of duration rather than on a mathematical theory that might be used only to index durations. The answer, supplied by evolutionary theory, will be along the following lines: given that certain relevant creatures on the cicada habitat have periodic life-cycles of *that* or *the other* duration, it is advantageous for the cicada life-cycle to be the particular duration it is, for this minimizes encounters between organisms. (Daly and Langford 2009, pp. 656–7)

There are at least two problems shared by both of these suggested lines of alternative explanation. Firstly, they are in tension with actual scientific practice. Even once biologists had good explanations for the long duration and periodicity of cicada life cycles, they remained puzzled about why these periods have the particular lengths they do. And there is good evidence, based on what they write and say, that this puzzlement only arose because of the fact that both of the known period lengths are *prime*.[81]

A second problem is that the alternative nominalist explanations are simply not as good as the number-theoretic explanation. The main reason for this is that they lack the *generality* of the original explanation. Indeed, they seem overly specific in two different ways. Firstly, the nominalist explanation rests on facts about one kind of thing (e.g. sticks), and it gives no reason for thinking that it will apply to other, different kinds of thing (e.g. time intervals). In other words, the nominalistic explanations lack *topic generality*. Secondly, any change in the numerical parameters requires that another exhaustive, case-by-case verification be carried out in order for a corresponding optimization claim to be established. Even if we can use sticks to demonstrate the optimality of 13 in one case and the optimality of 17 in the other, these separate demonstrations do not permit any predictions to be made about likely life-cycle durations in other

---

[81] See Gould (1977).

ranges. This argument works similarly for explanations based on detailed ecological histories. Thus the nominalistic explanations also lack *scope generality*.[82]

7.3 Mathematical Concept-Preserving Hard Road Fictionalism

The lesson from the previous section is that the concept of primality is central to the cicada explanation, and that it cannot be eliminated without undermining the generality of the explanation. Broadening the moral, this suggests that it may often be the case that particular mathematical concepts are indispensable to the mathematical explanations in which they feature. And this leads in turn to a second form of Hard Road fictionalism which aims to preserve the mathematical concepts involved in mathematical explanations in science, while eliminating the mathematical theories in which they are customarily embedded.

These more ambitious Hard Road fictionalists set their sights on paraphrasing the actual mathematical results that are appealed to by a given mathematical explanation in science. In the case of the original cicada explanation, this means paraphrasing Lemma 1. An example of this second approach can be found in Jonathan Tallant's (2013) paper, "Optimus Prime". Tallant uses mereological apparatus to formulate definitions of the key terms involved in the Lemmas, including coprimality, primality, and lowest common multiple. This allows him to express mereologically (and thus, he argues, nominalistically) the content of Lemmas 1 and 2.

In arguing against a concept-preserving Hard Road fictionalist of this sort, the platonist has a couple of potential lines of objection. The first is to raise specific worries about the nominalistic purity of the apparatus that is utilized. The second is to argue that providing nominalistic paraphrases of the core mathematical results is not enough: what is also needed is nominalistically formulated justifications of these results. In other words, it is not just the Lemmas but also their *proofs* which need to be reproduced. The platonist's thought here is that it is not legitimate for the nominalist to help themselves to nominalized results if they cannot non-question-beggingly furnish the grounds for these results.

Responding to this latter point leads to a second kind of mathematical concept-preserving Hard Road fictionalism. The goal in this case is – for each legitimate example of a mathematical explanation in science – to provide nominalistic paraphrases both of the mathematical results involved and of any additional mathematical apparatus appealed to in the proofs of these results. A good example of this approach can be found in a 2011 paper by Davide Rizza.

---

[82] See Baker (2017) for further elucidation of topic generality and scope generality.

Rizza uses axioms for measurement theory, first presented by Suppes, which allow the core results needed for the basic explanation in the cicada example to be proved without quantifying over any mathematical entities.[83] As with Tallant's framework, the platonist may raise questions about the nominalistic purity of Rizza's supporting apparatus. There is also the issue of the "piecemeal" nature of any such Hard Road fictionalist project. How extendable is it – in theory or in practice – to other examples of mathematical explanation in science that may utilize very different mathematical apparatus, and thus very different core mathematical concepts?

7.4 Mathematical Theory-Preserving Hard Road Fictionalism

If the platonist successfully insists that mathematical notions, of appropriate scope and generality, cannot be successfully reproduced in isolation from the mathematical theories in which they are standardly embedded, what then for the nominalistically inclined Hard Road fictionalist? Is there any remaining room for maneuver? Perhaps, for even if it is conceded that number-theoretic notions are essential to the explanation, the critic may argue that number theory does not necessarily carry commitment to numbers. The aim is to show how nominalistic underpinnings can be provided for our number-theoretic explanations while still retaining these explanations.

It is worth noting the striking – some might say strikingly counterintuitive – nature of this latter claim, effectively that mathematical objects are dispensable from *pure* mathematics. In pursuit of establishing this thesis, various more or less elaborate nominalizing strategies have appeared in the philosophical literature. Some introduce extra operators, for example the possibility operator of Geoffrey Hellman's modal structuralism.[84] Others loosen constraints on what counts as a well-formed formula, for example by working in a base logic which allows countably long combinations of truth-functional operators.[85] On this issue, we have little to add that goes beyond the broader debates concerning the effectiveness of these different nominalist projects. In each case, the two crucial questions concern, firstly, whether the proposed framework is adequate to reproduce the functions of the platonistic mathematical theory it is replacing and, secondly, whether the extra apparatus invoked is nominalistically acceptable.

Because this approach focuses on pure mathematics, in some ways it floats free of the specifics of the Enhanced Indispensability Argument. Indeed, essentially the same approach can also be implemented against the original QPIA version of the indispensability argument. In one respect, perhaps, shifting the

---

[83] Rizza (2011, pp. 106–9). [84] See Hellman (1989). [85] See, for example, Melia (2001).

context of the debate to the Enhanced Indispensability Argument favors the platonist. By focusing on explanation, and especially on inference to the best explanation, the bar is set higher for the nominalist. If a proposed nominalistic alternative is not as good an explanation as the platonistic original, then the original inference to the best explanation is not undermined.

8 Conclusions

A drawback for the platonist of upgrading from the Quine–Putnam Indispensability Argument to the Enhanced Indispensability Argument is that it makes the Hard Road easier for the nominalist to pursue. This is a calculated risk taken by the platonist side in return for strengthening the indispensability argument against the – arguably more threatening – Easy Road. Nor are all versions of Hard Road fictionalism made less daunting, as we saw in the case of the mathematical theory-preserving Hard Road fictionalism discussed in the previous section. However, it is definitely the case that new options for Hard Road fictionalism are opened up once the focus moves from a general theoretical role to an explanatory role, and from the theory-level indispensability of mathematics to the indispensability of mathematics for individual explanations in science.

Fifty years on from Putnam's first explicit formulation of the Indispensability Argument, the shift in attention, from indispensability *tout court* to explanatory indispensability, matches two more general shifts in the philosophy of mathematics. The first shift involves the gradual fading away of the view, often implicit, that the "real" philosophy of mathematics is the philosophy of *pure* mathematics. In this respect, the sustained interest in indispensability-related issues is part of a broader array of questions concerning how, where, and why mathematics is so successfully applied to the concrete physical world. The second shift is toward increasing interest in the philosophy of mathematical practice and away from more narrowly philosophical concerns. This move toward greater engagement with actual practice – and actual practitioners – is not confined to the philosophy of mathematics, but can also be seen in the philosophy of science. The debate engendered by the Enhanced Indispensability Argument fits well with this latter trend, since much of the focus is on specific case studies that have been extracted from actual scientific practice.

Finding more such case studies, preferably from a diverse array of scientific subdisciplines and involving a diverse array of mathematical apparatus, is likely to be one way that the indispensability debate will be advanced in the coming years. Another way is by making progress on several still-open questions. What is it for mathematics to "carry the explanatory load" in a scientific explanation, as opposed to merely being an indispensable part of the overall explanation?[86] How might the logical gap between the indispensability of mathematics and the indispensability of mathematical objects be bridged, if indeed it can?[87] And, finally, what is the precise nature of a mathematical explanation of a physical phenomenon?[88] To date, we lack a satisfactory general philosophical account of mathematical explanation in science. If such an account could be developed, then this might pave the way for a version of the Indispensability Argument that combines the grounding in scientific practice of the Enhanced Indispensability Argument with the ontological force of the original Quine–Putnam one. Indispensability-based considerations would thus remain a powerful basis for mathematical platonism.

---

[86] See, for example, Saatsi (2011).

[87] In other words, the (potential) gap between the truth of mathematical claims and the existence of mathematical objects. For a presentation of the (Frege-inspired) counterargument, see Linnebo (2017, p. 10).

[88] See, for example, Lange (2017).

References

Azzouni, J. (1994), *Metaphysical Myths, Mathematical Practice*, Cambridge University Press.

Azzouni, J. (2000), "Stipulation, Logic, and Ontological Independence," *Philosophia Mathematica* 8, 225–43.

Baker, A. (2003), "Does the Existence of Mathematical Objects Make a Difference?" *Australasian Journal of Philosophy* 81, 246–4.

Baker, A. (2005), "Are There Genuine Mathematical Explanations of Physical Phenomena?" *Mind* 114, 223–8.

Baker, A. (2012), "Science and Mathematics: The Scope and Limits of Mathematical Fictionalism," Book Symposium, *Metascience*, 21, 269–94.

Baker, A. (2016), "Parsimony and Inference to the Best Mathematical Explanation," *Synthese*, 193, 333–50.

Baker, A. (2017), "Mathematics and Explanatory Generality," *Philosophia Mathematica* 25, 194–209.

Balaguer, M. (1998), *Platonism and Anti-Platonism in Mathematics*, Oxford University Press.

Bangu, S. (2012), *The Applicability of Mathematics in Science: Indispensability and Ontology*, Palgrave Macmillan.

Blanchard, O. (2002), *Macroeconomics* (3rd ed.), Prentice Hall.

Burgess, J. P. and Rosen, G. (1997), *A Subject Without An Object*, Oxford University Press.

Cheyne, C. (1998), "Existence Claims and Causality," *Australasian Journal of Philosophy* 76, 34–47.

Colyvan, M. (2001), *The Indispensability of Mathematics*, Oxford University Press.

Colyvan, M. (2010), "There is No Easy Road to Nominalism," *Mind* 119, 285–306.

Colyvan, M. (2019), "Indispensability Arguments in the Philosophy of Mathematics," in E. Zalta and U. Nodelman (principal eds.) *Stanford Encyclopedia of Philosophy*, https://plato.stanford.edu/.

Craver, C. (2014), "The Ontic Conception of Explanation," in M. Kaiser, O. R. Scholz, D. Plenge, and A. Huttemann (eds.), *Explanation in the Special Sciences*, Springer, 27–52.

Daly, C. and Langford, S. (2009), "Mathematical Explanation and Indispensability Arguments," *Philosophical Quarterly* 59, 641–58.

Daly, C. and Liggins, D. (2011), "Deferentialism," *Philosophical Studies* 156, 321–37.

Duhem, P. (1906/2007), *La Théorie physique. Son objet, sa structure*, Vrin.

Field, H. (1980), *Science Without Numbers*, Princeton University Press.

Field, H. (1989), *Realism, Mathematics, and Modality*, Basil Blackwell.

Field, H. (2016), *Science Without Numbers* (2nd ed.), Oxford University Press.

Franklin, J. (2014), *An Aristotelian Realist Philosophy of Mathematics*, Palgrave Macmillan.

Goles, E., Schulz, O., and Markus, M. (2001), "Prime Number Selection of Cycles in a Predator-Prey Model," *Complexity* 6, 33–8.

Gould, S. (1977), "Of Bamboos, Cicadas, and the Economy of Adam Smith," in S. Gould (ed.) *Ever Since Darwin: Reflections on Natural History*, Norton.

Hellman, G. (1989), *Mathematics Without Numbers: Towards a Modal-Structural Interpretation*, Oxford University Press.

Hellman, G. and Shapiro, S. (2019), *Mathematical Structuralism*, Cambridge University Press.

Knowles, R. and Saatsi, J. (2019), "Mathematics and Explanatory Generality: Nothing but Cognitive Salience," *Erkenntnis*, 86, 1119–37.

Landau, E. (1958), *Elementary Number Theory*, Chelsea Publishing Company.

Lange, M. (2017), *Because without Cause*, Oxford University Press.

Leng, M. (2010), *Mathematics and Reality*, Oxford University Press.

Leng, M. (2021), "Models, Structures, and the Explanatory Role of Mathematics in Empirical Science," *Synthese* 199, 10415–40.

Lewis, D. (1991), *Parts of Classes*, Blackwell.

Liggins, D. (2008), "Quine, Putnam and the 'Quine–Putnam' Indispensability Argument," *Erkenntnis* 68, 113–27.

Linnebo, Ø. (2017), *Philosophy of Mathematics*, Princeton University Press.

Maddy, P. (1992), "Indispensability and Practice," *The Journal of Philosophy* 89, 275–89.

Maddy, P. (1997), *Naturalism in Mathematics*, Oxford University Press.

Maddy, P. (2007), *Second Philosophy*, Oxford University Press.

Maddy, P. (forthcoming), "Reply to Paseau," in J. Kennedy (ed.), *On the Philosophy of Penelope Maddy:Set-theoretic Foundations and Naturalistic Methodology*, Springer.

Malament, D. (1982), "Review of *Science Without Numbers*," *Journal of Philosophy* 79, 523–34.

Marcus, R. (2014), "How Not to Enhance the Indispensability Argument," *Philosophia Mathematica* 22, 345–60.

Melia, J. (2000), "Weaseling Away the Indispensability Argument," *Mind* 109, 455–79.

Melia, J. (2001), "Reducing Possibilities to Language," *Analysis* 69, 19–29.

Melia, J. (2002), "Response to Colyvan," *Mind* 111, 75–9.

Meyer, G. (2009), "Extending Hartry Field's Instrumental Account of Applied Mathematics to Statistical Mechanics," *Philosophia Mathematica* 17, 273–312.

Molinini, D. (2016), "Evidence, Explanation and Enhanced Indispensability," *Synthese* 193, 403–22.

Morrison, J. (2010), "Just How Controversial is Evidential Holism?" *Synthese* 173, 335–52.

Paseau, A. C. (2005), "Naturalism in Mathematics and the Authority of Philosophy," *The British Journal for the Philosophy of Science* 56, 399–418.

Paseau, A. C. (2007), "Scientific Platonism," in M. Leng, A. C. Paseau, and M. Potter (eds.), *Mathematical Knowledge*, Oxford University Press, 123–49.

Paseau, A. C. (2012), "Practitioners First," Book Symposium on *Mathematics and Reality* by Mary Leng, *Metascience* 21, 282–8.

Paseau, A. C. (forthcoming a), "Trumping Naturalism Revisited," in J. Kennedy (ed.), *On the Philosophy of Penelope Maddy:Set-theoretic Foundations and Naturalistic Methodology*, Springer.

Paseau, A. C. (forthcoming b), *What is Mathematics About?* Oxford University Press.

Pincock, C. (2012), *Mathematics and Scientific Representation*, Oxford University Press.

Planck, M. (1950), *Scientific Autobiography and Other Papers* (trans. F. Gaynor), Williams & Norgate.

Putnam, H. (1967), "Mathematics without Foundations," *The Journal of Philosophy* 64, 5–22.

Putnam, H. (1971), *Philosophy of Logic*, Harper and Row, repr. in his *Mathematics, Matter and Method: Philosophical Papers* 1 (1979), Cambridge University Press, 323–57.

Putnam, H. (2012), *Philosophy in an Age of Science*, M. De Caro and D. Macarthur (eds.), Harvard University Press.

Quine, W. V. (1951), "Two Dogmas of Empiricism," *Philosophical Review* 60, repr. in his *Quintessence: Basic Readings from the Philosophy of W.V. Quine* (2004), R. F. Gibson Jr. (ed.), Harvard University Press, 31–53.

Quine, W. V. (1970), *Philosophy of Logic*, Prentice Hall.

Quine, W. V. (1981), *Theories and Things*, Harvard University Press.

Quine, W. V. and Goodman, N. (1947), "Steps Towards a Constructive Nominalism," *Journal of Symbolic Logic* 12, 105–22.

Resnik, M. (2005), "Quine and the Web of Belief," in S. Shapiro (ed.), *The Oxford Handbook of Philosophy of Mathematics and Logic*, Oxford University Press, 412–36.

Rizza, D. (2011), "Magicicada, Mathematical Explanation and Mathematical Realism," *Erkenntnis* 74, 101–14.

Saatsi, J. (2011), "The Enhanced Indispensability Argument: Representational versus Explanatory Role of Mathematics in Science," *British Journal for the Philosophy of Science* 62, 143–54.

Strevens, M. (2011), *Depth: An Account of Scientific Explanation*, Harvard University Press.

Strevens, M. (2020), *The Knowledge Machine*, Allen Lane.

Tallant, J. (2013), "Optimus Prime: Paraphrasing Prime Number Talk," *Synthese* 190, 2065–83.

Urquhart, A. (1990), "The Logic of Physical Theory," in A. D. Irvine (ed.), *Physicalism in Mathematics*, Kluwer.

Vineberg, S. (2018), "Mathematical Explanation and Indispensability," *Theoria* 33, 233–47.

Wetzel, L. (2009), *Types and Tokens*, MIT Press.

Woodward, J. (2003), *Making Things Happen: A Theory of Causal Explanation*, Oxford University Press.

Yablo, S. (1998), "Does Ontology Rest on a Mistake?" *Proceedings of the Aristotelian Society* 72, 229–61.

Yablo, S. (2000), "Apriority and Existence," in P. Boghossian and C. Peacocke (eds.), *New Essays on the A Priori*, Oxford University Press, 197–228.

Yablo, S. (2005), "The Myth of the Seven," in M. Kalderon (ed.), *Fictionalism in Metaphysics*, Oxford University Press, 88–115.

Yablo, S. (2012), "Explanation, Extrapolation, and Existence," *Mind* 121, 1007–29.

Acknowledgments

We are grateful to the series editors Penelope Rush and Stewart Shapiro for the invitation to write this Element, to three anonymous Cambridge University Press referees for comments, and to Sam Baron and Sorin Bangu for feedback on an earlier draft. Alex dedicates this Element to Marta, whom he cannot do without.

Cambridge Elements ☰

The Philosophy of Mathematics

Penelope Rush

University of Tasmania

From the time Penny Rush completed her thesis in the philosophy of mathematics (2005), she has worked continuously on themes around the realism/anti-realism divide and the nature of mathematics. Her edited collection *The Metaphysics of Logic* (Cambridge University Press, 2014), and forthcoming essay 'Metaphysical Optimism' (*Philosophy Supplement*), highlight a particular interest in the idea of reality itself and curiosity and respect as important philosophical methodologies.

Stewart Shapiro

The Ohio State University

Stewart Shapiro is the O'Donnell Professor of Philosophy at The Ohio State University, a Distinguished Visiting Professor at the University of Connecticut, and a Professorial Fellow at the University of Oslo. His major works include *Foundations without Foundationalism* (1991), *Philosophy of Mathematics: Structure and Ontology* (1997), *Vagueness in Context* (2006), and *Varieties of Logic* (2014). He has taught courses in logic, philosophy of mathematics, metaphysics, epistemology, philosophy of religion, Jewish philosophy, social and political philosophy, and medical ethics.

About the Series

This Cambridge Elements series provides an extensive overview of the philosophy of mathematics in its many and varied forms. Distinguished authors will provide an up-to-date summary of the results of current research in their fields and give their own take on what they believe are the most significant debates influencing research, drawing original conclusions.